Here I am, Lord…

…Restless Nights

Other books by Sharron Dorst ...

Family, Friends , and Just Plain Thoughts

Here I am, Lord…

…Restless Nights

Sharron Dorst

RADIANT HEART PRESS
An imprint of HenschelHAUS Publishing, Inc.

Milwaukee, Wisconsin

Published by
HenschelHAUS Publishing, Inc.
Milwaukee, WI
www.henschelhausbooks.com

ISBN: 978159598-854-6
LCCN: 2021940355

Dedication

This book is dedicated to three Pastors and their beautiful wives.

Ed and Mary Ruth Kolbe of Arlington, TX.
They were the ones who really encouraged me to publish
my poems. My first book was published in 2015 and is called
Family, Friends and Just Plain Thoughts.

Bob and Jenna Wallace of Tyler, TX.
They have always inspired me and appreciated what I wrote.
They are the type of people who make you
want to be a better person.

Roger and Sandy Olsen of New Glarus, WI.
They started up a group called Synergy that inspired me to start
writing more poems and prayers for the Lord. They were my
sounding board on what to write.

I love each and everyone of them so much and
their friendship means the world to me.
All three of these couples are shining examples of God's love.

I'm sorry to say Mary Ruth Kolbe, Roger Olsen, and
Jenna Wallace have moved on to join our
Maker in Heaven above.

Table of Contents

Prelude

This book was inspired by a meeting group at our church called Synergy. Synergy is a way to communicate with the Lord whatever way you want. You can sing, wave flags, sit and meditate, read your Bible. We have people who do adult coloring books. We have people who will do healing prayers for you. I write poems that the Lord gives me and I read them to the group. We have a couple of people who paint pictures and draw when they are there. We always have someone playing and singing hymns during the full two hours that we meet.

The majority of the prayers in this book were inspired by this group. Others were thoughts and ideas the Lord gave to me. Some of these poems were given to me while I slept; all of a sudden I would wake up in the middle of the night and get up and write what I had been given in my sleep. So that is why this book is entitled *Restless Nights* because of those nights. My sincere hope is that you enjoy this book. My greatest wish is that maybe something I wrote will inspire you or help you deal with something that is going on in your life.

Thank you, God, for giving me the words for all of the things I wrote in this book.

—Sharron Dorst

A Lady of Grace

Her beauty is the first thing you see
It surrounds her like a spotlight from above
It is a beauty that shines from the inside out
She walked with the Lord proud as can be
To her husband Herman she was the perfect mate
She's was always there beside him with a helping hand
Their love radiated out for all to see
To her children she was the greatest gift they had ever received
She taught them how to love, and to live in the Lord
She told them to be the best that they could be
Her grandchildren thought that she was so cool
She came to all the games they played at school
To her friends she was always there showing that she cared
She is someone we all wanted to know, she just seemed to glow
Her kindness and sweetness are what I adored
She was a valuable treasure to her family, friends and church
She was a lady in every sense of the word
God has a smile on His face when He thinks of Jean
I know that she was my mother-in-law's BFF till the end

Alvin

Mary Lou was the glue that held your pack together.
But you were the leader of the pack who showed them all what
love was and how to share that love.
You both paid it ahead in your lives to anyone
who needed anything at anytime.
You showed everyone how to walk and talk like the
Lord wanted you to do.
You always loved your fellow man.
You were kind- hearted and did good deeds,
had compassion for others.
These things will be remembered by many
for a long, long time to come.
Losing your parents is never something that we are prepared for.
That loss leaves such a huge space in our hearts and our lives.
Just knowing that he was so admired, respected and appreciated
in his community. A man with morals and good values.
Who you can always value as having been your father
and your children's grandfather.
A man you can always be proud to have called DAD.
Such a shining example for his huge extended family to mold
themselves after in their walk with the Lord.
Just remember people will always remember him
with a smile on his face.
He lived a good life and was a God-fearing man.
He and Mary Lou are united in Love again.

Alzheimer's

One of the cruelest diseases anyone can have. Having known several people who have experienced this illness tears at my heart.

To have lived a good and wonderful life, full of memories and then slowly you start forgetting things. Most of them are small things so you don't really notice at first that it is happening. Then you start forgetting more and more things, but you don't panic it just part of growing old. We all get some of that as we get older so no big deal. Then slowly it gets worse with each day. We try not to panic when we think of what it might be. We put off asking our doctor if we possibly have Alzheimer's. Some Doctors will just tell you that it is stress and don't worry. If your doctor says that, you might think about finding yourself a new doctor, especially if you are 50 and above.

Sometimes it starts out with something as simple as forgetting your sign-on for your computer that you use every day at work. Then it keeps growing and growing forgetting more and more. Maybe you can't remember the names of some of your relatives. But that's ok because they are in old photos and passed away many years ago. Once it starts, this disease is irreversible; some drugs can slow it down but nothing stops it.

Sometimes you write notes to yourself about things you do on certain days to help you remember. Those notes eventually are the only way you function each day. You can watch a TV show and an hour later watch the same show and tell people that it is new and you haven't seen it before. It will eventually get to the point that you do not remember you have eaten a meal two hours ago and go looking for something to snack on; you will do this after every meal all day long. One day, you may wake up and you cannot remember how to do the laundry. If someone writes you a list on what to do to wash and dry your laundry, your life can go on.

For people going through this, life becomes so frustrating because they can't remember anything, especially all their daily chores. Why won't people leave them by themselves? Why are they telling me what I can and cannot do? Why won't they let me cook anymore? Probably because you have put water on to boil and forgot you did it and almost started a fire in the kitchen.

Learning to live your life always surrounded by people watching you and trying to protect you and keep you from harming yourself is a challenge. You may eventually go for a drive one day and then you can't remember how to get home, so you have to call someone to come help you. So now they will no longer let you drive your car for fear of your getting lost again.

Short-term memory loss is the first phase of this disease and may gradually change to not being able to remember what you had to eat for breakfast. Some people's disease progresses to the point that they do not recognize members of their own family when they come to see them. That is the saddest thing if it reaches this stage.

In the first stage they forget some things but not all of the time, then it goes on to forgetting more and more. In this stage, you will be asked 20 times a day or more what day it is. At this stage, just learn to be patient, patience will be your greatest gift to whoever you are taking care of. They really don't remember what day it is no matter how many times you tell them.

In dealing with someone with Alzheimer's, try to remember what things they did when they were younger. These memories should still be there and you can possibly get them interested into something they used to do when they were younger. Maybe they drew or painted, maybe they wrote stories. See if you can tap into those memories to help build a better relationship with them and a better life for them. My fathers greatest fear is that he would get Alzheimer's like his sister had. She was one of the unfortunate ones who forgot their families.

Sometimes patients get mad or angry for no reason at all. That is a side effect of the disease and no one has any control over it. Always make sure that if you are taking care of someone full-time with this disease that you have plenty of friends and family to help you. You will need to take breaks from your patient in order to maintain your patience. It is just as frustrating to you as it is to them, so beware of this. Pray for God to help you care and to guide you through this time of your life. Keep God in your life; He will be a great helper to you.

Anita

You are such an amazing servant of God. You have lived a life that was full of challenges. Having lost your father at an early age left a big hole in your life. Since we are all Daddy's little girl, this loss left you vulnerable. You didn't have a man to assess your boyfriends and help you find a good man worthy of your dad's approval. So that happening may have had a big impact on your adult life.

You married young to a man who became a pastor. You had eight beautiful children, all very gifted. Some are musically gifted, others have the gift of working with their hands doing gardening. They have all used their gifts well and are all servants of the Lord. Granted they have had challenges in their lives but the Lord has helped them through those challenges.

It was a hard time for you when your marriage ended through no fault of your own. Your mother and your faith in the Lord helped you move on after this happened.

Your biggest loss after that was the loss of your youngest child, which still haunts you to this day.

The Lord introduced you to a wonderful man who had a lot of the same interests as you. You both sing and love music which is a great passion to you both. You both have big loving hearts to help others in whatever way you can. I would say you are caregivers in one way or another. Life has brought you two closer still since your marriage and the challenges you have faced.

The loss of your sister Melanie was such a crushing blow to your whole family. She was the "get-er-done" person. When she called all of her kids and your kids to come help; they all showed up for fear of her wrath.

Then when things seemed to be going smoothly, your mother was diagnosed with Alzheimer's. Now more decisions to be made as to what is best for Mom in her future. You and Stephen chose to keep your mother at home and you would move in with her and take care of her for the rest of her life. The greatest gift that you can give anyone is the gift of yourself. You will always have peace in your future life because of that decision. Mom's safety is your number one priority and nothing is going to be allowed to happen to her. You will do your best to keep her healthy and safe in her daily life.

Taking care of someone with this disease is a test of patience because patients slowly lose their short-term memory in a lot of cases. This means they don't remember things that were said a day or two before, so you do a lot of repeating things that you have said before—things like what day or time is it over many many times in the same day. This will be one of the hardest things you will ever do in your life with a lot of good days and bad days. But after, you will have a lot of wonderful memories that you will remember in your future.

You are such a blessing to God for all of the wonderful things that you have done in your life. You have been and still are a wonderful wife, Mother, grandmother, a loving and caring daughter and sister. Best of all you are such a precious friend who has walked with God and can help others when they need it. God's blessings shine brightly over you. You are an amazing woman of God.

Are you an Optimist or a Pessimist?

What way are you in your walk with God? Are you an optimist who believes that things will get better? Do you look at problems or situations in your life as stepping stones? If you follow them and take your time that all will be well. It is just another step that needs to be taken to get where you want to go. It is just one of life's little bumps that we all have to deal with.

We walk our walk believing that there is nothing our Lord cannot bring us through. Believing that our God who brought His people away from persecution and slavery is still here. Believing that He is here today. We just cannot physically see Him, but we can feel Him. We can feel His love surrounding us and keeping us safe.

We believe that whatever we give to Him, He will take care of it for us. We know that if we earnestly and humbly ask for His help that He will be there. He will take our burdens from us and shoulder them for us.

We ask and expect that our Savior will be there for us. I believe that we will all have problems from time to time, but I know that He is there to help us deal with them. Thinking positively that our belief will conquer anything and everything. Thank you for being a powerful God.

Or do you always believe that something is going to go wrong. That your Heavenly Father is there for others but not for you. Is your faith not strong enough to believe that all things will be well. That we are just meant to wish and hope for naught. That He really doesn't care; He is only there for every one else. When we ask for something, He doesn't respond because of something that maybe one of our parents did.

Do you believe that He is punishing you because of them? Do you read your Bible and follow God's word or do you read it and forget it as fast as you read it? You as a pessimist don't wait to believe; you look for excuses to fault the Lord. You are forever climbing mountains when you could be walking on a flat road.

Don't you ever get tired of finding ways to doubt your religion. Of looking down your nose at those who believe in the Lord? Envying them for the good things in their lives?

So which are you? An optimist or a pessimist?

You have the power to change the way you think. But will you? Or is it His joy, peace, happiness, and His love that you are looking for?

Asking for Help

How many times did you need help and never asked for it? What held you back—fear, anxiety, shame or just plain stubbornness?

Why do we find it so hard to ask for help? We don't want people to look down on us. We don't want to admit at times we really do need help. Some time it is just our own pride.

Asking for help is not a sign of weakness. It is what the Lord wants us to do.

Like falling off of a ladder when you should have had someone holding it to prevent this from happening. Lifting things that are too heavy, causing us to pull a muscle or a ligament. If only you had swallowed your ego and asked for help.

God doesn't look down on us when we ask for help. It makes Him proud of us for putting our fears and worries aside. He always wants us to reach out to Him for help.

Whether its some big complicated problem or just a little nudge reminding us about a vital ingredient in a recipe, without that ingredient whatever we were going to make wouldn't have turned out properly.

We are so afraid of what others will think of us if we ask for help.

Without asking, you may never learn that a lot of people have walked the same path you are walking. Their wisdom and guidance will make it so easy for you to move on. We need to step aside and stop being our own worst enemy.

Desiring and asking for help makes God smile because He sees that we are moving closer to Him. He wants us to reach out to others for inspiration or guidance.

Reaching out past our comfort zone allows us to be bigger and stronger people. Knowing our strengths and weaknesses makes us more rounded individuals.

So put aside your fears, worries, and doubts and know that God is with you always just waiting for you to ask for His help.

Blind Trust

This is the one thing that the Lord wants from us. We can't see, feel, or touch Him physically but we believe in Him. This is what He asks of us in our walk with Him.

It is so easy to say you believe when He tells you the answer. But it is a totally different thing when you just totally know and believe that God will grant your request. It is a done deal, not "I hope so" or "maybe He will" are your thoughts. This is the blind loyalty that we give to Him every day as His followers.

It is so comforting to know this during our darkest hours. To give it all to Him and know that His will be done. When you remember that He so loved us that He gave His only child so we would be sin free. That is the greatest sacrifice of all to give someone you love so that they can benefit from it.

What a supreme sacrifice that was. All He asks us to do is just trust His love for us. He doesn't say, "Believe in me and I will think about it or I might do it." Ask in prayer and supplication, believing that He hears you and will bless you. In the game of Pin the Tail on the Donkey, we blindly believe when we are blindfolded that He will guide us to the poster.

That applies to everyday life. Why does one person get a disease and his brother or sister doesn't. Maybe with this pandemic we are meant to learn that we need to take a closer walk with Him. Maybe He wants to show us some things in our lives we need to work on.

I have always looked at sad or bad things in life as learning experiences. Are you going to step up to the plate and change your life or are you going to sit down and feel sorry for yourself.

Hopefully we recognize this situation for what it is—a message from the Lord. It is so easy to believe when you can reach out and touch something, but believing in something you can't see or touch is the hard part. If we are really lucky, we were introduced to the Lord as a child.

By reading the Bible, we develop a deep relationship with Him. But it is much harder to do if you never read His words. I was much older when I really learned about Him and His word. I believed there was a God , but I never knew all of the things He does for me. I never knew the true depth of His love for me.

After having survived several accidents, heart surgery, cancer, and the loss of most of my family, I know that He has always been there, loving and protecting me. He is always there every day, guiding me to do the right thing.

It is very easy at times to turn away from Him and lose our way. But that path sometimes leads to disaster. Stepping back and trusting in Him again will lead you back to your true mission.

Totally loving and believing in the Lord is one of the scariest things you will ever do. Reaching out and doing something new is always scary, but His love makes us believe that we can or will do it.

The Blizzard of 2011

This was one of Mother Nature's greatest shows.

I sat on an enclosed porch for hours watching the snow go flying by. It came in gently like a lamb. Now the 50 MPH winds hit us with a real slam. Blowing so hard, it was a wonder to see. I tried my hardest to see the tree across the driveway.

The drifts started small. I watched them as they moved around. I've never before seen so much fury in the wind. But I have seen the destruction from a mighty wind. Watching it spiral higher and higher, moving like a sandstorm with a mighty blow dryer.

The amount of snow you can see deceives. Small piles in some places, and other drifts that you couldn't believe when you see. Hearing the wind as it howled on by, we prayed to God that we will all come out alive.

When people talk about white-outs, we think they are nuts. But watching the wind blow on by, you see why the fuss. Like Mother Nature's other disasters once is more than enough.

Trying to recoup and recover is going to be tough. Some lost power, so they were so cold. Some lost a lot of food when the power was out for so long. There was such a mess to clean up.

Sometimes, ice and rain was mixed in. Trying to walk in the storm was really a trick. We can't wait until the end of this ugly storm, which dropped 17 inches of snow in its wake.

We can't wait for spring, so we can be warm again.

Choices

I can't say that I ever consciously thought about what things to do or not to do. I have always done what I thought I should do or what felt like the right thing to do.

When I was a child, I spent a lot of time with our elderly neighbors talking to them or helping them to do something. Sometimes I would go get their mail at the post office or run to the local grocery store for them. I never questioned why I did these things. One neighbor was in a wheelchair and I went to visit with him. It didn't feel strange; it just felt right.

Helping others is such a major part of me and my life. There was never any thoughts of rewards or payoffs. I just wanted to help whenever and however I could, it made me feel good. This has continued throughout my whole life. My ways to help might have been financial, offering a shoulder to cry on, or providing a simple helping hand when needed.

When I got older, some things I did for a different reason. When my mother was terminally ill, I went home for two and a half months to take care of her. I knew deep in my heart it was something I had to do. If I hadn't done this, I would be guilt-ridden the rest of my life.

We all have to live with the consequences of our actions.

When you have to make a choice like this, just ask yourself if you can live with yourself if you choose wrong.

So 11 years ago, when my baby brother was terminally ill, I didn't blink an eye about helping to care for him and did this for eight months straight. This was a labor of love and my brother knew I would be there for him.

I now can live the rest of my life feeling good about the choices I made and not feel guilty for not doing the right thing.

Starting a year after my brother passed away, I started volunteering for hospice, sitting with patients who didn't have long to live. I would sit with them so that their loved ones could get out of the house. Sometimes, I do end-of-life sitting with patients who only have hours to live. I have gotten more out of this than I have ever had to give.

My mother and brother both had hospice care, so this is my way of paying back for the care they were given.

Christmas Past to Present

I remember the wonder and glory of family Christmas time in the past when all the members of our family were there.

On Christmas Eve, the excitement kept building all day knowing what was going to happen later. That day the time just seemed to creep along because we were so anxious for nighttime to come. We couldn't wait to eat and get the table cleared and dishes done. Christmas Eve was for immediate family only. After everything was clean and put away, we would sing some songs. Then we got to open our presents since we went to midnight mass after that. Passing out presents and cleaning up all the paper was quite chaotic but so much fun. After all of the gifts were opened, we played a while and then had to get dressed and go to church.

We would get up early the next day. Usually my father and I were the early birds so I could finish making the dressing, stuffing the turkey, and getting it in the oven to cook. Each year, my mother and her sister alternated cooking Christmas dinner. So after the turkey was in the oven, we would start peeling the potatoes, preparing the vegetables and salad, awaiting the big meal.

By the time my aunt, uncle, and their kids, plus my grandmother, showed up, the meal was almost ready. When we all sat down to eat, no one made a sound—we were all so busy eating. I remember one year halfway through the meal, my dad discovered that he didn't have any turkey on his plate; we had so much food and his plate was piled that high with it.

After we ate and did the dishes, we would sit at the dining table and play penny ante poker, which was so much fun. Later that day, we would have leftovers for supper and some pumpkin pie. Being with family is what it was all about.

Even after I got married and had kids of my own, coming home to my family at Christmas time is what we did. We were stationed in Bad Kreuznach, Germany for three years, so at Christmastime, our house was full of friends and people who worked with my husband. They were substitutes for our family but just as welcome. Even at other holiday times when we were back in the States, we always had people over for Christmas if we could not be with ours. A house full of people, laughter, and good cheer is what counts.

My parents died when I was in my late thirties and early forties, so since then, having family and friends near make the season bright. But now things are sad for me, as all of my family have their own families and they all live far away and they have demanding jobs that keep them from coming our way.

My closest sibling has a family that gets together. My baby brother passed away ten years ago. My twin sister lives in California and has a family of her own, so she is never here. They are all I have left of my immediate family.

My children live in Oklahoma, Florida, and Alabama, too far to just drop by. So this year has really saddened my soul that I don't have any of my family to share the holidays with. My husband has family but it was not the same as what I grew up with. There is no fun or cards or joy in their home, so going there is something to endure. Now his parents are gone and one brother has passed away, so his family doesn't come around anymore. Sometimes his younger brother comes to our house. But I am so unhappy that all of them are gone and no longer here for me to feel their love. I hope that everyone appreciates their family time and treasures it always. I would give everything I own to have one more Christmas with all my family members who have passed on.

Covid-19

Who would have thought that this time would have ever come? A virus so eluding that the world was stunned. Spreading from country to country via plane or boat. Why some people get it and others don't. Why do some people recover and others don't? Why did this happen and when will it stop?

Going to the store and the shelves are empty of most things. I couldn't imagine of such a thing. But seeing is believing and not just a hunch. All of the things we have all taken for granted. Everything changed in the blink of an eye. Not just one race, religion, city, state, country or nation—this has affected the whole world. Its not over yet and the death toll is incomprehensible. It doesn't matter your age or your sex and I'm hoping you were lucky and given the test. But some people couldn't get it for a reason or to, mostly it was because they were short about a million or two.

People losing jobs and their whole world is changed. People being isolated for months because they were on a ship at sea. The virus affected some; others were exposed and no ports would let them dock. People being told to stay at home if they were over 65. This is the worst thing if you are alone no one to come and visit you, or no one you can go visit.

People dying and nothing their family can do—no viewing or funerals. No hugs from family and friends. No one to hold you while you grieve being there alone and that is the end. Such heartache and pain to never be able to see that person again. No closure coming, counting the time until this nightmare ends. No lunches with friends, no going to exercise at the gym. No movies or parties with all of our friends. No beauty shop appointments to get our hair done. No social activities to have some fun. Putting distance between people wherever we go.

No Sunday church services for you to attend. Here's a new thing: YouTube has your church. Start texting and calling to keep in touch with your friends. Even a simple card can mean so much when you are so isolated from others. Isolation can have such terrible results, mainly depression. We all need and crave attention and companionship in one way or another.

I imagine that my parents and grandparents suffered through some of the same things during WWI and WWII, not to mention the Great Depression.

Here we thought that we had come so far, but guess what this virus showed us how unprepared we really were.

So the only thing I know is true that trusting in Jesus will definitely get us through. Take time to read your Bible every day for encouraging words you can pray. Pray for everyone, not just those people you know; we all need prayer. Help people in whatever way you can and always be willing with a helping hand.

If someone had told me such a thing would happen in my lifetime, I would have told them that they were out of their mind. The effects of this virus will take a long time to recover from. But who knows what time will bring. Hopefully we will be better because of it. Praise the Lord.

Covid 19 Pandemic Truths

This time has been the worst of times and the best of times.

The worst has been all of the people who have died from this virus, and not being able to have a wake or funeral for your loved one. The isolation this virus has forced on us. Shortages and price increases to purchase food and products. Having to constantly wear a mask every time you leave your house. Breathing is really hard to do in a mask. All of the people who have lost their jobs. Tons of stores and businesses that have closed. Not being able to visit with our loved ones. Not being able to travel to see loved ones.

The best part is we have had time to spend with loved ones. Time to be with and enjoy our children. Time to enjoy doings things with our partner. Time to find creative things to do as a family and be safe. More time to read our Bible and say more prayers to God. Time to sit and reflect on all of our blessings. Time to think and praise the Lord for our lives. Time to appreciate everyone in our life.

Time to tell everyone how much you love them.

This poem will be published in "
Best Poets of 2020, Quarantine Edition.

Dad's Passing

My greatest fear when I was growing up was losing my mom and dad. That was the only real fear I had as a child. Even when I married and had children of my own that was still my greatest fear.

My mother had a lot of medical problems so I always thought she would pass first. When my father complained about stomach pain shortly after returning from a 40th Anniversary trip to Hawaii, we had gotten for them. He was complaining of stomach pain, which we thought may be from a big belt buckle he always wore after such a long plane trip. His doctor referred him to a clinic to have testing done. He checked in Monday, on Tuesday, they did his test, and Wednesday, they told my mother they were 90 percent sure he had liver cancer.

Mom called my sister and me and told us to come home quickly. Our sister picked us up at the closest airport to the hospital on Friday night. We talked to my father Friday night and all day Saturday. Saturday night he went into a coma.

Monday morning, they did a biopsy so we could code him DNR (Do Not Resuscitate). The biopsy came back inoperable cancer. We got the results about noon on Monday and by 5:00 that afternoon, he had passed away from heart failure. We were there holding his hand when he took his final breath.

All of us were in a state of shock that it happened so quickly. My father was 61 years old and had been healthy all of his life. I never knew you could go from healthy to deceased in a week. My father passed one month before his first great-grandchild was born, so he never got to meet and know all six of his great-grandchildren and nine great-great-grandchildren.

My father was a machinist by trade; he could tear an engine apart and put it back together in a flash. We were used to seeing an engine hanging on a tree branch while he worked on it. He was a great carpenter and built many things in our house. He taught us girls about tools and what each one did. He would be proud of all of the carpentry work we girls have done.

He was preceded in death by his son Jerry. His survivors included his wife Phyllis, daughters Lynne, Sharron, Sheila and son Bob. All of us were under 38 years of age. He is loved and missed.

Diamond in the Sky

You were a star for the world to see
Goodness and kindness radiated out from thee
Helping others was your main concern
Something that all of us should learn
Your friendship was a gift to my everyday life
But many times you had so much strife
Your smile was like a ray of light
Always there through good times or blight
You were always the light of Alvin's life
He was so proud to call you his wife
Thru good times and bad you made him complete
Having you at his side was ever so neat
Your gift to him of 3 beautiful girls
Was just what he needed to complete his daddy world
Your daughters are so different but loaded with fire
Protecting their family brings out their ire
You were the magic that held them firm
Your abounding love gave them room to learn
It was an honor and privilege to call you a friend
And those special feelings will never end
Even though you are no longer here
You're with our Lord and He is holding you so dear
The gap you leave will never be filled
But the memories we have will always have top bill
Until we see you in heaven above
You will always have all of our love
So spread your wings and fly
Because you are a diamond in the sky

Do You Believe?

Do you really believe or is it all just lip service?
When God said do unto others as you would have them do
unto you, do you do that every day?
When you see someone in pain or distress, do you go and try
to comfort them, or do you turn your back because
you don't know them?
What would you like someone to do to you come
and hug you or walk away?
When someone says something unkind about you, do you
retaliate back or say a prayer that God will forgive that person?
When hard times fall like a job loss or losing a loved one, do
you go to your knees and pray, or do you become angry and
blame the Lord?
When we feel like others don't like us, do we become resent-
ful or do we ask the Lord to help us change?
When our life is crazy, do we blame everyone else or do we
sit down and think of things we can do differently?
Are we reading and taking in God's word or are we forgetting
His word as fast as we read them?
If we are not willing to take His words and grow,
then why read them?
God wants us to learn, grow, change and better ourselves.
That is the reason for His messages to us. He wants us to change
our lives to His way, loving each other, treating others like He
treats us. He wants us to love one another in the same way He
does us every day.
The amazing part is that all it takes are simple things. The
simple kindness of holding a door open for someone makes them

do the same thing for someone else. Smiling at someone you pass
will usually have them smile at the next person they see.
Smile when you talk on the phone and the person at the oth-
er end of the phone will usually sense what you are doing.
Changing our life and our world can be done with baby steps
that mushroom into something bigger.
Just think that the Lord is always smiling down on us.
The greatest things start with just one step.
So just take that step to start the change
that God wants from us.
He will take over from that point on. Praise Him
and He will lead you.

Doctors

Some are good and some so so
I have known many good doctors
They are caring, concerned and they listen well
Others are so frustrating because they don't listen well
As a patient I get so confused
One doctor says that number is too high
Another doctor says that number is ok
So you as the patient have no say
Why can't they get together and agree on a number
One says you need to be back on your meds
The other says no you are fine off of the meds
They give you medicine for a problem they perceive you have
Then three months later when problems arise they disagree
They look at you like you're crazy
because this side effect cannot be.
It is not in their PDR drug book
But some side effects only affect a small group of people
so they don't count or get listed
Just because it's not listed doesn't mean it's not a side effect
So doctors need to stop and really listen to their patients
Then give serious consideration to what they are telling them
Some people know their own bodies much better
than any doctor does
If he is not willing to listen to me then he is not the doctor for me
Doctors do their best with all of training that they have
But they are humans just like us and can make mistakes
So think carefully when you select your doctor
Please stand up for yourself and get the right care.

Encourage or Discourage

What type of friend are you? Do you encourage your family and friends or do you discourage them.

When someone comes to you with a problem, do you listen to them and then tell them some encouraging words or scripture?

Do you do your best to help build their confidence in themselves?

Do you give them positive examples of what they can accomplish?

Do you also try to use encouraging words and examples from the Bible with little children? When they ask you for advice do you do your best to be a positive encouraging force in their lives?

Do you try to get people to read the Bible and learn that God is always there to help them? Sometimes just a simple little thing like a smile can brighten someone's day. Little do you know what that smile did for them or how far it will travel that day. A smile is such a simple thing but moves mountains, your smile will make them smile at someone and that person will smile at someone etc. That smile can travel around the world in a day.

Always try to be encouraging to people especially in these trying times? With all of the negativity in the world between Covid, people losing their jobs, and possibly losing their homes. Those are just a few and there are many more, so anything encouraging you can say to people will really help. It takes less energy to be a positive force and encourage people, so take the easy way. I would much rather people think of me as a encouraging friend, who is there when people need some hope in there life.

Or are you the discouraging person who is always telling people how dumb or stupid they are? Someone who is always discouraging people about their lives? Who when you ask them for advice all you get is negativity from them? They don't see anything positive so all they do with their lives is to discourage others from even trying something new. These are people who have never believed that the Lord does exist or that He can change there lives. Something went wrong in their life and no one helped, so to them, all is negative. There was no one there to pick them up and to encourage them to try again. They just received bad feed back from the people in there lives who mattered.

Think of the influence you can have on people who are growing up. When they see you encouraging people, that rubs off on them even if they do not realize it. But when you grow up with discouraging people, that is what you model your life after, not purposely but you follow the examples you have been shown.

I'm praying that you are the lucky one who is being raised by encouraging people. May God keep you on the right track in your walk.

Faith

Normally when you see this word, you think of your belief.

But today, that word is for something very different. It is for a little girl in the NICU unit at the hospital. She was born as a premature baby fighting for her life. She is aptly named because God's faith has kept her alive. He has been there every step of every day, clearing her paths and lighting her way. She has fought harder already to live than most people fight during their whole lives. Hearing of her daily struggles is like walking hand and hand with the Lord.

Just hearing her name brings a smile to my face because she is living proof of what faith can do. She is and will remain to be one of the Lord's chosen ones. He has a very special purpose in mind for her, Faith. Hearing her story inspires people, because we actually get to see our Lord at work. The miracles He is performing right before our eyes.

We know the Lord performed many miracles in the Bible, but that was a long time ago. So it is so wonderful to see Him performing some of them in our time that we can see.

Faith's life has been nothing but challenges, which has made her parents step deeper into their faith. He has been and will continue to be with you both on Faith's journey. God is holding you both during your trying times. The rest of the time, He is walking by your side and carrying Faith in his hands.

My prayer for you all is that God grants your every wish now and as Faith continues to grow. He has arranged surgeries when needed, and miracles for those that He could heal. He will continue to handle all of her problems as they occur. That her rough beginning built the strong foundation for her to grow on. That she will always have what her name implies: FAITH.

May her life bring others back to the Lord because she truly is a miracle. I hope that she makes others want to fight for life the way that she has fought for her life.

May God bless Faith and your family always and may you always sing His praises for the miracles you have seen in her life.

Find Me on My Knees

One of my greatest failures is not spending enough time on my knees praying to the Lord. I did a lot of that as a Catholic child.

The older I got, the less I did that because it really hurt my knees when I kneeled on them. Now I use the excuse of bad knees, but that is an excuse. I pray all of the time, but not while on my knees. I rationalize this by saying God hears my prayers, but does he?

So my question is that required for God to hear our prayers? I have had bad knees since childhood so I would move forward and lean on the next pew to pray in church. Because if that is the case, what do people in wheelchairs do when they can't kneel? I'm feeling that being humble in prayers is more important than being on my knees.

The older we get, the harder it is for us to kneel. So I beg the Lord to forgive me for not being on my knees. Most of my praying happens when I go to bed while I am lying down. Taking time to pray every day is one of the most important things we can do.

Putting your faith in the Lord is what He wants from us. Praying for others who need His help is so important. Praying for our pastor, our president, and anyone who leads us, for guidance in their lives. Keep them all on your life path for us, not their path doing what you want done for us.

Forgive Yourself

As humans this is one of our greatest faults
Learn to forgive yourself for all of the wrongs
you have done in your life
God doesn't want us to continually punish ourselves
He has forgiven us by His son dying on the cross for us
All we have to do is ask for His forgiveness
Either say it out loud, write it down but
get it out of your system
We error and make mistakes
We have to forgive ourselves
That seems to be the hardest thing to do
Why is it that God can forgive us but we can't forgive ourselves?
Do we think that we need to be punished?
We are flawed and imperfect people to begin with
We are predestined to mess up
Our Lord and savior is perfect, but we were not meant to be
By making bad judgments or poor decisions
we are meant to learn and grow
So God expects us to choose wrong sometimes
But as we will learn and grow
hopefully we will mess up less and less
God doesn't want us to beat up ourselves
He wants us to learn and grow in His words
The more we learn and pray to Him to help us and guide us
The more we grow as humans and as God's people
The fewer and fewer mistakes we will make in our life
As we grow up we will learn how to better keep ourselves
from doing wrong things

We will learn to turn more and more
to the Lord for guidance
And if we happen to err, He is there to forgive us
It is so easy to ask for His forgiveness,
just say, 'I did wrong. Lord, please forgive me.
It is that simple.
So stop punishing yourself and just forgive yourself.

Forgiveness

This is the hardest thing God asks us to do, because He says if we cannot forgive, then how can He forgive us?

Forgiving someone who has hurt us either by deed, words or by an act seems almost impossible. But in order for us to be forgiven, we have to learn to forgive those who have wronged us.

Our first thoughts are "Can't do that. No, not going to happen. I was the one that was hurt. After all they did to hurt me. Next comes they never have apologized to me. They are not sorry for what they said or did."

After a lot of thought and praying, Well, maybe I can do that. OK, I am going to do it. Now how do I do it?

I recently decided to forgive several people in my life. I sat down and wrote out what I was forgiving them for. After I wrote it all out, I was ready to tell the people involved. But the more I thought about it, the more unsure I was that I should tell them. Because by telling them everything I felt, I could very easily hurt them very much. That was not my intention, so back to the drawing board I went.

Also, what if they don't feel they have done anything wrong? What then?

I finally asked my pastor's wife what would she suggest I do under the circumstances. She also felt that it was a good idea to just say it to God and leave them out of it. So I did just that and it made me feel a whole lot better for having done it. I forgave and I didn't have to hurt anyone in the process.

The forgiving part is the easier part but the forgetting part will take a lot longer, but it will happen eventually. In order to be what God wants us to be, we have to do this. Also to bring peace and contentment to our life we need to do this. If this were an easy thing to do, we would all rush out and do it right away. But since it's not, we hold on to our hurt with all we have, not realizing that we are hurting ourselves.

We are keeping ourselves from having a much closer relationship with God. That close walk with the Lord is after all what we want occupying our lives. We do not want nor do we need negative thoughts that the Devil keeps in our head. By saying "I forgive you," we are freeing ourselves and beating the Devil at his own game. Bye, bye, Devil.

I asked one of the people I needed to forgive what would they say if I said, "I forgive you"? Their response was a surprising, "I guess I would say 'Thank You'." My response was, "You're welcome."

Life seems a lot easier since I told this all to the Lord and forgave the people I needed to.

Is withholding your forgiveness adding anything to your life? Or is it taking something from your life? Is withholding it making you closer to God or further away from Him? Is it encroaching upon your relationships with people because you won't forgive? Eventually you may find yourself all alone because you refuse to forgive.

Don't wait until you are standing over their casket to finally forgive them, because they will never know and maybe have gotten some peace out of knowing that you forgave them. Some people are not strong enough to be the first person to forgive someone else. As some people surely know that not doing the right thing when they should, can and will eat at them the rest of their lives.

God's Canopy

O what a beautiful canopy He created for us.
He gave us blue skies to look at
The sun to warm us and to grow flowers and vegetables
The best canopy is his love for us
He is always there to guide us along the right path
To love us no matter what is happening in our lives
Encouraging us to stay strong and uplifted
His protection is always covering us
His canopy can block anyone trying to harm us or lead us astray
As long as He is in your life you do not need to fear anything
His armor will protect us from whatever the devil tries to do
His canopy is more protective than any umbrella
anyone could ever make
By pouring out your prayers you add to His canopy
Singing His praises makes His canopy shine
Worshipping Him just strengthens His canopy
What can you do to add to God's canopy over you?

Grandchildren—Things I Missed

A good friend of mine just became a grandmother for the first time the other day. She is so excited and over the moon. I am so jealous of the time that she will have with this baby. I have six grandchildren in three separate states.

When we lived in Ft. Sill, OK, we had our first grandchild and she lived with us for about six months. Her father joined the Army and his first duty station was Germany, so when she was six months old, she and her mother left for Germany.

My next grandchild was born in El Paso, TX, and we lived in Ft. Lauderdale, FL. So no special moments with this child, who lived too far away. When my third grandchild was born, we were still in Ft. Lauderdale, FL. They lived in Ft Sill, OK, but moved to Florida to live with us. So I had several years with this child to make special memories. They lived with us for three years then they got their own apartment. We didn't live that far apart so we got to see him at night and on weekends and then, we moved to Dallas, TX.

Our next grandchild was born in Ft. Sill, OK, which is three hours away from Dallas. We had our fourth grandchild for one week when his mom had to take a class for her job. After that, we only got to see our three grandchildren in Oklahoma on weekends, holidays, or whenever their parents came down to our house. Since my husband and I both worked, we didn't see them often.

Our fifth grandchild was born in Ft. Lauderdale, FL., and we had moved to Slidell, LA by then. So we didn't see much of this child—only on vacations and holidays.

Our sixth and last grandchild was also born in Ft. Lauderdale and we were still in Slidell, LA. So same thing—no special memories, just visits on holidays and vacations.

As of this day, my oldest grandchild is 37 and my youngest one is 15, so they are grown up and I have very few special memories of them. The oldest three have children of their own and they all live in Oklahoma. Now I have nine great-grandchildren there, and I don't get to see them but twice a year when I go to there to our daughter's house. Then I get to see my great-grandchildren. Sometimes my daughter and her husband come here and bring different great-grandchildren with them to visit.

Because we moved so much with my husband's career, I missed out on the chance of having tons of memories with them.

My friend lives 20 miles away from her grandchild, so she will have a lifetime of memories with this child. I am so glad that she will be there to collect all of the special memories that they will make together.

If I had a do-over in my life, I would have stayed where my grandchildren lived so I could spend more time with them and have more memories. Fortunately, they live by their parents so when I take my big trips each year, I get to see them and spend time with them. They all love me and love the time that I get to spend with them and their children.

All of my grandchildren and great-grandchildren call me by the same name: NANA. It warms my heart to hear my great-grandchildren call out to me when they see me. I love them all and miss them all so very much.

Wishing things had been different but enjoying the time I have with them all. Thank you, Lord, for all of theses precious memories.

Great-Grandchildren

I have been blessed with nine great-grandchildren so far. There are still three unmarried grandchildren so there could be more.

Kourtney is the oldest. She is blonde, just like her mother. She is also sports-minded, like her mother was, and also loves to play baseball. She is a typical teenager busy with school, sports, and keeping up with her girlfriends on the phone. She is 15 years old.

Braden is next in line. He is a typical boy who likes sports. He wants to know about tools and what they are used for. He loves to help do things outside. He also likes to cook, playing on his laptop and cell phone. He is twelve years old, four months shy of 13 (at the time this book was written).

Dylan is next in line and the younger brother to Braden. Dylan is a total tech guy, playing games on his laptop. He loves playing with cell phones and making all sorts of faces appear. He is the opposite of his brother: no sports, no outside work of any kind. He is eleven years old, four months shy of twelve.

Colt is next in line. He is my only red-headed great-grandchild—not sure if it comes from the Irish or the Scots. He is definitely not a sports type or outside work guy. Another one of those tech guys. That is most kids today. They love to play games. He will be eleven years old in November.

Kamryn is next in line; her big sister is Kourtney. She also is blonde, like her mom and her sister. She also loves to play baseball like her mom and her sister did. So safe to say she loves sports. She will be ten in October.

Easton is next in line and he is a half-brother to Braden and Dylan. He is the only child I know who loves going to school. He cant wait for school to start each year. He has brown hair and small in size but is growing slowly. He loves playing on his laptop and playing on cell phones. He is a tech guy but has some sports tendencies. He is seven years old, three months shy of turning eight.

Keeley is next in line and her big brother is Colt. She is a brown-headed little girl, not red-headed like her brother. She is in kindergarten this year so has a lot less play time this year. She is petite in stature but she will grow. She is a typical little girl who loves to play with toys and dolls. She is five years old.

Kayleigh is next and she has three half-brothers: Braden, Dylan, and Easton. She is blonde and petite in stature but she will grow. She loves anything to do with the movie *Frozen*. She loves watching movies on her laptop and playing with cell phones. She is in pre-school this year and loves it. She is four years old and three months shy of turning five.

Zayne is the last so far and his big sister is Kayleigh. He also has half-brothers—Braden, Dylan, and Easton—so he is the end of the line. He is a bubbly, roly-poly little baby. He is so cute when he smiles and is growing steadily. He has light brown hair like the rest of the gang. He will be six months old in three weeks.

I am so proud to have all of theses great-grandchildren and I love them all so dearly. I can't wait to see what they will all grow up to be. May God bless all of you and always be with you as you grow up. May He guide you and protect you as you grow up. Always know that He always loves you, like your NaNa and PaPa do.

Healing for Our World

Lord, we ask You to heal our world. We know a lot of this is Your plans. But too much of it is not Your plan. We ask you to end Covid forever. Please provide food for all those who have lost their jobs. Please provide them with shelter, clothes, heat, and protection from the evil in this world. The good and bad that are happening now for are for people to learn and grow from. For people's hearts to open and expand to see You for the wonderful Lord and Savior that you are. For them to understand what it is that You want from us and what You want us to do.

Father, please take away prejudice, hatred, and evil from everyone. Please have people stand up and demand that You be put back in our schools and in our world. Don't let people tell us when and where we can pray to You. Where we can say Your name without fear of repercussions.

Lord, please open the hearts of everyone to see what they need to change their lives. Please continue watching over us and leading us to walk in Your path. Let us see and understand Your wishes and desires for us. Open our minds to understand Your messages and for us to respond to what You are telling us. We need to fully understand that what needs to be done will be done because it is Your will and not ours.

We need to turn to Him for everything in our lives. We are nobody without Him. We cannot do anything without His support. He needs to be a vital part of our everyday lives.

Hello, God

Me: Hello, God.

God: Hello.

Me: I just wanted to thank you.

God: For what?

Me: Your love.

God: But I love all my children.

Me: I know, but we don't tell you often enough.

God: Well, that is true.

Me: So, Thank you!

God: Is there something else?

Me: Yes.

God: What?

Me: Also for your guidance and leadership through my whole life.

God: I do this for all my children.

Me: I know, but I am so thankful that you always do.

God: Thank you, my child.

Me: Thank your for protecting me from harm all my life.

God: That is what I do for those who follow me.

Me: Thank your for clarity and wisdom when I needed it.

God: That is part of what a good leader does.

Me: I am just so thankful that you do it.

God: I want you to fully understand my word and teachings.

Me: That is why I try to read my Bible every day to learn more about you and what your wishes are for your people.

God: That is good.

Me: I try to do all of the things I have learned from the Bible.

God: That makes me smile.

Me: But sometimes I do a very poor job in faithfully reading every day.

God: All I ask is that you continue to do your very best.

Me: Thank you, God

God: You are always welcome, my child.

Me: Are you ever disappointed in us, God?

God: Sometimes, but I then remember that your are human and full of flaws.

Me: Do our failures upset you so much?

God: I know that you are easily led astray.

Me: Sometimes we are, but we try to do better and keep ourselves from committing sins.

God: I am so pleased that you make great efforts to change to please me.

Me: Your teachings are what we need to follow to be the persons you want us to be.

God: This is how you will get to spend eternity with me.

Me: Caring for all humans the way you care for all of us?

God: Yes, loving your fellow man just as I have shown you all to do.

Me: Thank you for the sacrifice of your son so that we can be without sin.

God: Jesus willingly gave His life so that my wishes for you were met.

Me: I hope that we would all have the same strength and courage as you displayed.

God: I am with you always on your walk through life. Just call out to me when you need me.

Me: But we don't call out to you enough, do we?

God: Sometimes, no, you don't.

Me: But there are many times you are carrying us, when life has struck us down with sadness.

God: Yes, many times I do carry you.

Me: Thank you for that.

God: My child, I love you so much.

Me: Don't you get tired of us calling to you all of the time for help?

God: No, I live to hear you call me.

Me: I'm sorry that we do not sing or call out our praises to you more often.

God: Concentrate on making a greater effort to do my will.

Me: Lord, I have learned through life that a lot of things that happen are meant to teach us some kind of message.

God: Yes, that is true.

Me: I know that we all need to work harder at what You want for us instead of what we want for us. Our greatest fault is that we want everything in our lives, in our way and in our time.

God: Yes, my child. Yes, you do, but you need to remember that all things are done in my time.

Me: We need to develop patience so that we learn to appreciate everything You give us.

God: Yes.

Me: We also need to recognize the gifts you have given us and use them for your good.

God: Yes, my gifts to you are special, so do not waste what I have given you.

Me: It has been nice chatting with you, Lord, because you are who I admire and respect most.

God: Sleep well.

Me: Yes, I will until my next sleepless night.

Highlights of My Life

In my early life at one time there were 8 of us,
but one died at birth
So that just left 7 of us here on God's glorious earth
My mom, dad, 2 brothers, 2 sisters and me
It was hard but we ran free
We lived in a very small town
Houses and friends were all around
We played all day all over town
Finding things to do was easily found
Those friends of our youth are here today
They know you so well there's nothing to say
Then came a horrible, horrible day
My oldest brother was taken away
In the blink of an eye, our lives were changed
Our parents felt so much pain and rage
Now our family was down to the six of us
Such a sad and lonely time for us
My personal defender has gone away
Now my two sisters can rule the day
So much changed for our brother who was seven
The brother he was just starting to know was in heaven
No older brother to help mold his life
Parents changed the rules for the rest of his life
A few years later we left the nest
I guess our parents got a rest
In my mid-thirties, my life stopped on a dime
Phone call from Mom, Dad having some tests done
It appears he might have cancer and we are all upset

Four days later it's cancer, so please come home
Came home Friday and by Monday he is gone
My greatest fear is staring me in my face
Losing my parents was always my fear
But life goes on and so do I but now there are only 5
We all thought that all would go on
Four years later we are losing our mom
We were too young to have experienced this
Now all that's left is my brother, 2 sisters and me
The losses keep coming in the next couple of year
Our grandmother and an aunt who I held dear
Our lives all changed from all of these events
We had all come through life's horrible test
More bad news in later years
I was diagnosed with breast cancer
So having a mastectomy would save my life
Several years later we are tested again
My husband had to have quad bypass heart surgery
and we did win
One year later my life fell apart for sure
Hurricane Katrina devastated our life
Five feet of water came into our house
The loss of everything was worse than a surgeon's knife
My doctor said you cannot live there
So we were homeless and lost the only house we had ever owned
Anger, rage, pain and depression became my life
I suffered for a year to regain my life
Six years later and we had moved back to Wisconsin to live
Phone call came saying my youngest brother was taken ill
He was in renal failure and needed to have his leg amputated
Flew him to a big hospital to have it done

Between his diabetes and other problems
these things would end his life
So for eight months I was with him daily at the nursing home
Watching him get thinner and thinner till he was gone
Back to those dark and lonely painful days
Grieving for someone I loved who was taken away
But I am at peace that I was there for him to the last
Because we shared a special bond that I know won't pass
Now the three of us are all that's left
Waiting for another one of life's test
The lessons I have learned from all my losses
have helped me to be who I am today
I feel fortunate that I could be with them when they needed me
No matter what hand you are dealt always choose life
Family and lots of friends will get you through the strife
While my guardian angel helps me with the lay of the land
Doing for others brings joy to my life
Always remember to pray to our Lord
God has been there holding me in the palm of his hand
I am fortunate enough to have a husband for 55 years,
Three beautiful children who have given me six grandchildren
Those six grandchildren so far have given me
Nine great-grandchildren
I can't wait to see what else the Lord has for me.

How Great He Is

I am just amazed that people actually got to see and talk to Jesus. He performed so many miracles right in front of them. They saw first-hand all the things He could do and did for them. But when He wasn't around, they reverted to Doubting Thomas. I am just dumbfounded by them. How could you be there and see it happen but still doubt?

We who have never seen Him or heard Him talk, believe in Him. We do see or have heard of miracles happening in our time. People who are told they have a terminal disease and people pray for them, then they go back to the doctor and he tells them their disease is gone—that is a miracle.

You are in a terrible car accident and walk away unharmed when everyone says you should be dead—that is a miracle.

Danielle, whose parents own Sugar River Pizza, was at death's door. Doctors said, "Say your goodbyes." Everyone prayed for her and the pastors prayed over her. She walked out of the hospital to live the rest of her life—that is a miracle.

But miracles nowadays aren't being hailed and celebrated or even spoken of in the press, because they say it doesn't sell papers. In Jesus' time, word of His miracles spread like wildfires.

When we hear about theses things now, we don't go, "Thank you, Lord, for that miracle." We just say, "Oh, it's wonderful that she is better."

Other people do not even acknowledge that this could happen. But we as believers praise Him for theses miracles. We know that if we believe in Him, He can do theses things even now.

That terrible disasters happen and sometimes there are only a few injuries when there should have been mass casualties—that is a miracle.

We are a lot like the people in the Bible. We see and hear of miracles but never acknowledge them or praise Him for them. We are so busy in our lives that we never stop and think about all of the miracles we have heard about or read about. We here on earth only know a small portion of what His greatness can do and does do.

The more we learn about His Word, the more we will become more aware of these things. He is always there for us. We need to live our lives with this belief. Believing—not just saying we believe because that is what others want us to say.

I know that if I ever saw Him perform a miracle in front of me, I could never forget it happened. I know it has happened and will never forget it. I am eternally grateful He was there walking beside me. Praise the Lord.

I Am Blessed

I have a husband of 55 years who loves me dearly. We have had our ups and downs but have always worked through them. I often wonder why he is still here because at times I'm not so dear. He doesn't complain when I pack up and leave and come back six weeks later. In fact, he tells me that that he knows my friends need me as much as he does.

I have three beautiful children I love to the moon and back.

My oldest one is April, who is my protective grizzly bear. You will get along with her as long as you don't pick on her mama. If you bad-mouth her parents, she will be after you. She is a caregiver and does whatever she can for anyone she loves. She has three children and nine grandchildren to fill up her life.

Dawn, my middle child, is my quiet one. Her claws will also come out if you mess with her parents. She has a beautiful spirit and a gentle soul. She has one son who is the apple of her eye.

Last is my son Scott, who loves to cook. He is a loving and caring person to all who know him. He is also very protective of his parents, so watch what you say. He has two children he spoils come what may. He loves spending time with his mama when she comes to town.

I am also blessed with a wonderful son-in-law who loves me to death. He is a loving, caring person with a huge heart. He loves my daughter with everything he has. He is the greatest grandfather to my great-grandchildren, who are not biologically his. He loves and protects them from the bottom of his heart.

I have six grandchildren I hold dear. Four of them are all grown up and have families of their own. The last two are still in school and have families to come.

Last but not least, I have nine great-grandchildren who totally love me. When I visit them, I park in a certain place and when
they see a car there they know NANA is here. They come running
into the house like the streets are on fire shouting, "Nana is
here." I don't get to see them often but they are the loves of my
life. They range in age from three days old to twelve years.

Now come my sisters, Lynne and Sheila, my twin. Lynne
lives in Illinois and I can see her whenever I want. Sheila lives in
California and I see her maybe three times a year. They are all I
have left of my family of seven: Mom and Dad, Jerry and Bob
have all passed on. Having lost so much, my sisters and I realize
how important family is. All of our family members passed away
too soon; our parents were in their early sixties, Jerry was 20,
and Bob was 54. So like the saying goes, blood is thicker than water, we really know is true. We look after each other even though
we are states apart, we cherish our friendship and hate being
apart.

Next are all of my friends east to west and north to south. I
love seeing them all as they fill up my soul. I feel their love and
that they really care and knowing this nothing else compares. No
matter how long I stay—one day or twenty—it's never enough.
They just ask when I'm coming back. I am always thankful to
hear from them and I hope and pray they all stay healthy. They
have been there for me through the tragedies in my life. They are
a very vital part of my life.

I'm Sorry

The most overused words in the world
The most apologized-for words around
If only we thought before we spoke
If we never spoke when we were mad
If we took the time to cool down before we spoke
Think of others feelings that we would hurt
Or someone's heart that we would break
We should never hurt anyone we love
Always think of others first
If we do the things listed above
we should never have to say those two words
After everyone is calm, sit down and rationally talk
Then no one has to apologize
Always think before you speak
Ask the Lord to silence your mouth
And give you a gentler spirit

Impatience

I find one of the greatest challenges in life is having patience.

It starts when we are born and growing up. We can't wait to crawl, then to walk, then to talk. Can't wait for Christmas or for Easter to come. Learning to read and write but always waiting for summer to come. To go outside and play, to go swimming in the pool, learning how to ride a bike or roller skates.

The older we get, we want to learn to play baseball or basketball, tennis, or some other form of sports. In high school, we get more freedom; we get to go to dances and football or basketball games. We hopefully find a boyfriend to take us places and maybe to the prom. We can't wait to get our driver's license and then we can get a car. Then we can't wait to graduate and get on with the rest of our lives. Some of us went on to college; others got married and had families. No matter what path our lives took, we couldn't wait for it to happen.

Our society has slowly turned into a throw-away society. We toss our marriages away instead of repairing them. Then a lot of people marry the same type of person they just got rid of and wonder why this relationship isn't working either. The saddest thing is that some people throw away their family and friends who love them and keep them grounded. Someone may have said something or done something that they can't forgive them for, so they toss them away also.

Our impatience shows the most when we are driving a car. We get angry when traffic is moving slowly. Some people literally get road rage and do some really stupid things. Sometimes, if we had just left a little earlier, we might not have had the traffic slow down. So sometimes a lot of this is our own fault because we become impatient. So sometime when we are caught up in traffic, we need to sit there calmly and ask the Lord what is it He wants us to see at that particular time. Maybe the delay is His way of keeping us out of an auto accident that is going to happen just up the road. We just need to relax and hold our tongue and temper when something happens. Just say, "Thank you, Lord, for this slow traffic or my running late."

We have all grown up with fast food, fast cars, and get-rich-fast ideas. Some people live in the fast lane and run with the wrong crowd.

Just ask God to help us change our lives to conform with His plans for us and give us the patience to await these changes.

In the Blink of an Eye

I went from having a fully furnished home, the first and only home I have ever owned, to a house that had had five feet of water in it. Everything was all ruined. I lost my car, all of my clothes except what I had in a bag, and a house full of memorabilia and memories. I lost the pillow that had been in my mother's casket. I lost the watch my father bought me in Hawaii before he died. I lost a bracelet and a note from my brother who passed away four years later.

The cause of all of this was HURRICANE KATRINA.

When we were finally allowed to go see our house, it was complete devastation. Garage doors were dented, the front door was warped so once opened, it would not close, and a back door that has been destroyed by rescue workers looking for survivors.

There had been five feet of water in my house. Furniture had been moved around and cabinets lay on their side. The only things we could salvage were paintings we purchased in Germany when we were stationed there, along with the crystal I also purchased there. I was able to salvage Precious Moments figurines that had been given to me by family and friends. The paintings were hung high enough so no water damage. The Precious Moments, crystal, and other figurines could be washed in a dishwasher to sterilize them. We were able to fill forty small boxes everything else was lost. Fifty-eight years of my life were gone.

Having to face starting all over again from scratch at my age was totally overwhelming. I went from being a happy person to someone living in a big, black hole. I lived in that hole for a whole year. Most of the time, I was alone as we only had one car and he worked in the evenings. I slept a lot of the time, trying to decide if I really wanted to remain on this earth.

A year after the hurricane, I finally decided to rejoin the world. Having a lot of friends I could call and talk to helped me get through this whole situation, I needed all of their love and support to get me back to living again.

If losing everything wasn't enough, our insurance company was screwing us. The only good insurance was the flood insurance we had purchased earlier that year. They tell you one thing and do just the opposite. So it just makes it harder to move on with your life.

The whole situation has left a really bad taste in my mouth. So I swore never to buy another house because of how badly they ripped us off. I can honestly say to this day that any kind of disaster in which people lose their lives or their homes still brings me to tears.

People do not understand the difference between willfully selling your home compared to it being taken from you. When you sell, you are prepared to leave it and move on. No one is prepared to have their home taken from them through no fault of their own. It's possible to get over, but seeing some other disasters brings some of those feelings back.

The last fourteen years have been a big adjustment period. Fifteen days after we moved to Janesville, Wisconsin, my mother-in-law had a massive stroke and passed away ten days later. We helped my father-in-law as he needed us; three years ago, we permanently moved in with him. It was a lot of adjustments on both sides but we were all willing to do what needed to be done. We added whatever we needed to the house to keep him safe. He passed away almost one year ago. He left us a beautiful house to live in and I cannot lay claim to it for fear of being ripped off by an insurance company again.

God carried me for a long time until I was strong enough to start walking by His side again. All the people I loved brought me back from that hole.

Don't ever give up; there is always hope. If we believe strongly enough, God will help us with whatever we ask of Him. But beware, He will also show you some things you may not like. Areas that you need to work on.

We walked through our own personal hell and came out better people because of it. No matter what happens to us, life goes on. So pull up your big girl or big boy pants and get back in the game, because life is worth living.

Isolation

The hardest part of the last three months under Covid-19 restrictions has been the isolation. Isolation is hard enough to endure during normal everyday life, because we have a choice of going out or staying home. The last three months, we have had no choice about isolating ourselves, because it has been advised and mandated by our governments.

If you are elderly or have various health problems, they pretty much mandated that we stay in and away from everyone, because simple things like going to the post office or grocery store can expose us to this virus.

Self-isolation can be horribly hard on people. As a society, we need contact with other people. When we do not get to go out and visit with friends, we have a huge void in our life that nothing else can fill. Of course, we can call or text our family and friends, but we need that human contact in our lives.

When we have this contact, we feel that we have some purpose and that we matter to someone. But without it, we feel useless and unwanted. In order for us to continue, we need this interaction. If we do not have it, some of us start feeling depressed. We start wondering why are we here and what good do we do. When such feelings start happening, it is not a good thing. Each day we can sink deeper and deeper into despair and start thinking of some really negative things.

We need to have things to look forward to every day, even if it is just that someone is going to call us and chat for a while. So please make it a point to go out of your way during these times and keep in touch with people. Your call or text may be the only thing they hear all day, but it can be enough. I try to text messages and positive thoughts every day to at least twenty people in our church to let them know someone is thinking about them. I try to give encouragement in the form of a prayer or verse.

Some days, I may just say, "Hi, wishing you a good day." Or reminding them that they are beautiful and that God loves them.

Knowing that we are loved and needed is what reading our Bibles does for us. God's word is always going to be a healing balm to our hearts and souls.

Don't let the devil get a foot in your front door. If you start feeling down, pick up your Bible and let the Lord guide your thoughts. His Word will show you that we are always in His heart and thoughts. So He should always be in our hearts and minds as well.

Thank you, Lord, for the words you give me and through me, so that they will help someone else.

Jerry ("Doc") and Gloria

Everyone calls him "Doc" because he was the chiropractor in the town where he lived for over fifty years. He treated many people with various problems in his practice. At times, he even treated some of the pets and farm animals. He loved helping people feel better and walk better. When someone came in and he asked them if their back bothered them and they said no, Doc would take his elbow and run it down their spine and watch them cringe. Then he would say, "I thought you said there was nothing wrong with your back."

For a man who would soon be 93, his sense of humor could not be beat. His mind is sharp as it can be, remembering his childhood he can still do. Telling about his time in World War II. The fun he had teasing his brother about the ways of the Lord. Good-natured teasing with Gloria, his wife, about various things in the Bible.

He constantly studied and questioned things in scripture that he didn't understand. He is an Elder at his church, so he was looked up to and sought out for advice. He has taught many Bible classes over the years to young and old. Teaching people about the Bible and the Lord are what he lives for.

Doc was what you would call a self-made man who had come from a hard childhood. Gloria was his perfect match; she was as fervent about her religious training as he was. They both taught Bible study classes. She was the light of his life. She had a glorious voice like the angels up above. Her joy and love of music were such a wonderful gift. Their walk with God was such an all-consuming love.

The losses in his life have been many, including his parents and all of his brothers. The death of his wife, however, left a very big void in his life. The loss of his middle son, Gary, was worse than going under the knife, that pain seemed to stay.

Jerry loved to go hunting for birds, fish, or deer. He loved the challenge of hunting with a bow and arrow. He loved to be on the water in his boat fishing, and loved cleaning and filleting them after that. But the funniest thing is that he didn't really care to eat the fish; he gave most of the fish away to friends.

Now you and Gloria are back together in Heaven above, Doc.

Joey

Your face lights up when you talk about doing His work
Your roots are grounded and your faith is secure
To see in you the joys you get doing his work
His spirit just radiates from you
Listening to you talk, people see His love
I know at times it was hard walking His way
Knowing that you knew others who didn't feel this way
I know that you have touched so many lives
But what stands before you will blow your mind
Take the lives you have already touched
and multiply that a thousand times
Nothing has prepared you for the great times ahead
Seeing so many new places and faces,
making so many new friends
God is walking beside you providing His light
Your heart has been chosen to do His work
You have the passion and desire to do this work
Being so young and knowing your way is surely a gift
All who meet you see the Lord at work
Hold firm and stand steady; God knows your worth
You make your parents very proud,
seeing their faith walking in thee
Wherever life takes you, He's protecting you
One of God's mighty warriors on earth for all to see
Be proud of yourself. You are a glorious young man.

Josh and Anne's Grief

We all exhibit our grief in different ways. Some people go totally quiet and never talk about the person they lost. To them, their loved one is gone and never to be discussed again. These people are ridding themselves of that person's possessions and that can't be done fast enough. I don't know if removing everything makes it easier to go through their daily lives.

Most people grieve the normal way, slowly, over time. It may take them years to get their loved one's possessions out of the house. They love to talk about the person they lost. Their loved ones remain a part of their everyday lives. They keep things to remind them of their loved ones; their memories are always a part of their lives.

I have experienced so much grief in my lifetime and keep mementos and memories of the people I have lost. Even though I have good memories of the people I have lost, each loss is harder and harder to get over. It takes so much out of me when I lose someone I loved; it just takes longer and longer to try to come back from the loss. I have lost parents, siblings, tons of friends, aunts and uncles. and some cousins.

But I have never lost is a child. Both my mother and grand-mother lost children in their lifetimes. I have so far been blessed not to have lost any. I had the privilege of listening to a father who lost his son about a year ago. The hardest part of that loss is that the child was a twin, so his brother is still alive. It is so hard to lose a child but to still have a child that looks so much like him still there for you to see every day. It is just human nature to think of that child every time you look at his twin who is still there, so trying to survive takes on a whole new meaning in their lives. It is almost impossible to forgot the child you lost when his twin is always there. At least most other people don't have living memories to try to deal with when getting over a child they lost. Listening to him talking about losing this child was so gut-wrenching.

I am very familiar with grief but hearing him talk about this child the way he talked about this son nearly destroyed me. Feeling his pain as he talked was so tangible. He was not afraid to show the depth of his grief. I don't know how he could stand before us and speak. He made us understand the depth of the loss he was feeling. How broken he feels and how God was showing him things so he could heal him and repair his broken heart. God was showing him how he felt when he gave his son to die on the cross for us. He showed him what it is like to have a father's heart and the grief he felt.

Dealing with grief is so hard and some people never get over it. To them, their life is over. Nothing will ever repair them so they give up.

The man's wife is still so broken that she cannot get up and speak of her loss. I'm praying that the Lord will send tons of healing grace and peace to these two wonderful parents so they can continue doing their ministry work in Your name.

But the one who doesn't have a big say is so confused and may someday be able to talk about this but for now doesn't know a lot or understand it all. Because it happened when they were so young, the surviving brother doesn't fully understand where his brother went and why. Yes, he has been told the brother went to Heaven to be with God, but doesn't fully understand the meaning of those words. He doesn't fully comprehend why Mom and Dad cry when they look at him for no reason. He may wonder what he did that made Mom and Dad cry. Why one day he had a playmate and the next day, everybody was sad and his playmate was gone.

Where did he go and what did I do that made him go away? When will Mom and Dad stop crying when they look at me?

That is sad because God loves them all so much and is there supporting them. He will bring them all through this time and give them a wonderful future.

Please don't ever give up as life is always worth living, even though the pain is unbearable. Your loved one wants you to move on and be happy. We never want the people we love to suffer and be unhappy. All we want is for them to be loved and to find happiness again after we are gone.

To everyone who has gone through grief, I hope that you are able to find some happiness on the other side of grief. Remember that God is always there holding us, loving us and carrying us when we need Him to. He is our strength to hold on to when times are hard and painful. Praise be to the Lord.

Laurie

Oh, how I miss the massages you used to give me. Your hands could do such magic to my bones. Your kindness and goodness stand out like a star. You have tons of compassion for your fellow man and it is easy to see. When you injured your shoulder, your whole world changed. You suffered through a lot of pain and discomfort. The pain you suffered, hoping to be able to use your arm again. The tears you shed when your plans fell through The frustration of trying to get the compensation due you.

My heart aches for all of the unfair things you have dealt with in your life. I love seeing the changes you have made in your life. Basically starting over again in mid-life. You pulled up your big girl pants and got on with your life. Finding a new job that is so totally different from your old one. Getting used to the weird working hours and trying to sleep. It took a little while but you finally did succeed.

The last few years have been like a really bumpy road. A few smooth places but definitely a lot of pot holes on the way. Your faith and love of the Lord have helped you get through the pot holes. The devil just loves to try to wreak havoc in your life. But having had a near-death experience, you know what Heaven really looks like, and you know that God is waiting for you.

You always ask me what you can do for me; you have done more than you will ever see. When I lost my brother, you were there with a shoulder to cry on. Anytime I needed to talk about him, you were there with a listening ear.

You have helped guide me through many other times in my life. Your upbeat spirit brings a smile to my face. You are a forever friend and a true confidant. You are there for me as I am there for you. You are a caregiver at heart, so receiving from others is hard for you.

You don't feel like good things should happen to you. But just the opposite is true; you deserve every good thing imaginable. My wish for you is that you can start believing in yourself and expect great things to happen in your life. You need to know that you can overcome any obstacle or climb any mountain, God is with you. Just believe in yourself and ask God to help you be all that He wants you to be. You are protective like a mama bear, loving like a furry kitten, tenacious like a vicious dog . You are like an Angel loving, giving, guiding and always there with a helping hand.

Life Experiences

It is so glorious to look back on your life experiences and what you have learned.

As a young child, I spent most of my time helping the elderly people who lived around us. Grocery shop, go to the post office or anything else they needed. That experience taught me to have respect for my elders.

Being one of five children born in the forties, we didn't have a lot of money. So I learned how to mend clothes, sew on buttons and darn socks. As teenagers, we detasseled corn so we could buy our own school clothes. I learned the value of hard work.

I learned how to plant a garden and how to freeze food from it. Valuable skills to know as I got older and had a family of my own. I knew how to cook, clean, iron clothes and do laundry at an early age. That taught me how to be self-sufficient.

I went to work in my twenties as a nurse's aide on an orthopedic ward at the local hospital. I got people up and helped put them to bed. We cleaned and straightened their rooms as well as giving them back rubs. I learned compassion for my fellow man.

I love doing minor house repairs like pulling up carpeting, and then putting down floor tiles in that place. Taking the hardware off of cabinets and either painting it or replacing it before putting it back on. Painting the interior of many family and friend's homes. I love painting because I can do it by myself and enjoy the peace and quiet while I am doing it. I love the feeling that I get when it is done and they are so happy to see it. I learned the satisfaction you can get in giving to others.

I took care of my mother and my brother before they both passed away. That taught me that the greatest gift you can give your family is caring for them in there time of need. Regardless of what it may cost you, that gift is priceless.

Having raised three children and been around my six grand children and visiting my nine great-grandchildren has taught me to be patient and loving. For the past nine years, I have worked with Hospice patients in their homes or in nursing homes. I occasionally do end-of-life with people who are near to leaving this earth. I have learned kindness for my fellow man.

I can see pain in people's faces when I look at them. I try to do something that will let them know that I see their pain. I love doing good deeds for others as that nourishes my soul. I love listening to people who need someone to talk to. I appreciate being asked for my advice from others. I feel that whatever I say to them are words that the Lord has given to me. All of my poems and prayers are ideas that the Lord wants me to write about.

I hope that what I write can soothe, comfort, and give someone hope that they are not alone. My writing has also helped me get through so many life tragedies. It has helped me voice things that I could not say out loud. It has helped me release anger, grief, sorrow, and pain but it has also helped me show love for so many people who meant a lot to me. Sometimes it was for people who have gone through the same things as me. I have learned the gift of caring and sharing.

The one constant in all of this is that God was always there loving, protecting and guiding me. I am hoping that something I wrote said or inspired someone else or comforted someone or gave them courage to change some things in their lives. I have learned at some times in our lives we need to be a little daring.

Life's Natural Disasters

None of us is ever prepared for a natural disaster. No matter how hard we try to live a good life, we are not ready to experience the unexpected.

Hurricanes can be tracked but you still have several different possible locations; at the last minute, they turn and go somewhere else. People have become lax. So when given warning, they ignore it most of the time because it goes somewhere else, so some people do nothing to prepare. So with unpredictable locations it is difficult to be ready; you can only just try.

Tornados can be tracked and warnings issued, but they hit here and rise up and hit somewhere else. How can you be prepared when they can change direction at will. Or when they come after dark and you cannot see them coming.

Tornadoes, like hurricanes, can change their paths at anytime. Even though we do our best, disasters still happen.

Flooding is the side effect of the first two storms. If it comes slowly, stalling out for days so much flooding happens, because where else can all that water go?When streams, ponds, and small lakes overflow their banks, no one can stop or control the damage that happens. No way can you know or control where all that water is gonna go and how badly the damage will be. Raging water cannot be stopped until the storm is gone and the rain quits. It can take weeks and sometimes longer for all of that water to go away and all the water goes down and back into where it came from. So water being in your home can do a lot of damage that takes a long time to dry out. Many times, your home can be fully or partially enveloped with water.

Forest fires are so deadly they just keep spreading from area to area. Sometimes they just have to burn themselves out. Sometimes with enough people, hoses and planes, they are controlled and eventually put out. No time, no notice, no way to prepare. All of the precious mementos of people we loved, things that cannot be replaced because the people are in heaven above. In so many of theses disasters, one minute you have a house and the next it is gone.

Theses disasters leave behind such terrible waste. It can be minor damage that is easily fixed or total devastation and your house is gone. If your house is flooded, it needs to be gutted, dried out and then rebuilt. No where to live, no clothes to wear, no money to start to fix and repair your house. If you are an older person having to start all over again is a tough pill to swallow.

To a lot of people, insurance wasn't there or wasn't enough to cover your repairs. You had to have flood, fire, hurricane special insurance for these disasters. If you did have insurance, you are going to get hit again because you will only get reimbursed about 30 to 40% of what you claimed. Everything is discounted so much, plus you cannot remember every little thing that was in your house.

For example, if you have a washer and dryer in your garage, sorry to tell it won't be paid for as your garage is not considered part of your house. After all of that has happened and all that you have lost. Now your insurance company will deliver another heart-wrenching blow. After all of the years you faithfully paid your premium, they will now screw you. So some people never get enough money back to repair or replace what they have lost.

It is so hard to deal with the loss because it was taken from you and you had no choice. Others cannot understand how this feels, unless you have experienced one of these disasters. Normally, you make a decision to sell your house and move all of your possessions intact. But this wasn't your decision and most of your possessions were ruined and lost. Everything you valued was just taken and forever lost. People say they are sorry and sympathize but they can never identify with the loss that you feel.

In some instances, on top of losing the house, clothes, furniture and your car, you have also lost your job as it was destroyed too. So here you are no house, no job, no money minus a car. So your feeling the lowest you can feel. There isn't much that can top that unless you lost a loved one or a pet.

You are totally crushed, desperate for help from anywhere. Where do I go, where can I stay for a while, where do I get money to live on and survive? The saddest thing is that most people are relieved that it is you and not them. So hopefully you belong to the Lord. He is the only person who can help you survive what your life has become.

If you know someone who has gone through one of these disasters, you may now know how they felt. If you know someone who has experienced any of this, give them a hug and a shoulder to cry on. It helps to know that some people really do care. Thank you, God, for carrying me in your arms and helping us to recover from these emotional scars and giving us hope.

Losing an Older Brother

The first nine years of my life, there were four of us. Jerry would have been 13, my sister Lynn 11, and my twin and I would have been 9. My older brother was my protector in our group and my older sister was my twin's protector. So if I did something to my twin sister, my older sister would pick on me. Then I would tell my older brother and he would pick on my older sister.

So growing up, I always had someone taking care of me. I was 16 when my brother was killed in a automobile accident. It was hard losing him because I lost my brother and protector at the same time. I felt abandoned and alone with no one to have my back. I got picked on more because he wasn't there. I have missed out on seeing him get married and having a family of his own. My children never got to meet him and he never got to meet them.

Jerry was only 20 when he passed away. He was a great brother and a good role model also. We had lots of fun playing baseball and football in the neighbors yard. Playing croquette in the other neighbors yard. All of the childhood memories are all I have left. Jerry was a jock; he played baseball, football and track were his sports.

My brother died instantly, so there was no time to be with him and say goodbye. His wake lasted for two nights. All of his classmates, teammates, and even rivals he played against, were there. Then there were our older sisters' classmates, our class-mates and all of the people we all grew up with. All of my parent's friends and co workers. Plus all the other relatives of ours. The line of kids stretched for blocks and it is still to this day one of the longest wakes I have ever gone to.

Jerry was well liked and respected for his abilities. I still miss him and it has been 57 years. Can't wait to see you again.

Losing Friends

As I sit here waiting for a call I don't want to get
Another loved one passing, someone else to miss
More tears to shed for the pain and loss at hand
The older I get,
the more times I'm called on to go through this again
Every time I think it will be the last, it's not.
For most of them I know that God is holding out His hand
For some I'm hoping that they will finally find some rest
In many cases the end is a welcome relief
For some leaving this earth are really dragging their feet
One day they were healthy and the next they were gone
Others got sick and it really lingered far too long
Sitting with your loved one day after day
watching them slowly slip away
Praying there was something you could do to change the outcome
Knowing that whatever comes will be done as God's will
It is so very hard to sit and watch the people you love suffer
No matter if they are young or old the cry is the same don't go
But if you really love them, tell them it's ok to go
God's waiting for them and we will see them again.

Loss

Waiting for a call to come
Wishing it could be undone
No good news would it bring
Just pain and sorrow and other things
My heart aches with just the thought
Of another friend that I have lost
I know that God is waiting for her
Job well done my wonderful girl
Her suffering has ended no more pain
Now she is free and ready for fun
Our pain is just beginning
Our loss is so fresh
Tears keep falling with the tightness in our chest
Memories assail us of good times and bad
Birthdays and Christmas times all in the past
They will always be near in our memories and hearts
Stories that we can tell to the generations to come
Remember all the good times the laughter and the fun
Remember with love and pride the values she instilled in you
The long hard path she walked and won
Her never-give-up-and-get-it-done attitude
Family and friends were her pride and joy
Kindness, compassion and a giving heart
Loving and caring for children filled a void in her life
The word stranger never crossed her mind
She had a care-giving heart to do good deeds
Now you can relax and let God take care of thee
She'll be ever loved and ever missed.

Marvin

You are another name to put on that list of people I miss
You are such a easy person to love
You radiate God's love with your welcome smile
You truly care about those you love
You sit and listen when others need to talk
But if asked you have a lot of wonderful thoughts
The compassion and love you have for your family
is just full of glee
The love you all have for each other inspires me
The wisdom and knowledge you have shared with me
You are always there with a smile and a hug
Welcoming me when ever I come on by
The wonderful meals we have shared
Wonderful memories to fill our heads
The laughter we have all shared
Your wonderful support for the things that I wrote
Your faith and belief are what appealed to me
Getting to know was as easy as a breeze
The Lord works through you and your love attracting others like
a moth to a bulb
You show patience, kindness and love to all you meet
You are a wonderful teacher of God's words from above
I'm sure people loved working for you
Your children and grandchildren dearly love being around you
You have set wonderful examples for them all to aspire to be
The kind and gentle way a man shows his love
The great morals and values you stay true to in your life
I know you can't wait to see our Heavenly Father above
Till we meet again in eternity. Like you said to me,
"See you next and I will save you a seat."

Melonye Ann

I had a friend called Melonye
Who wasn't much taller than me
She had long blonde hair and beautiful eyes
Her smile could easily light up the sky
She was a devoted and loving wife
Robert was the man who lit up her life
Their love was a beacon of light
That would light up the sky at night
She was the proud Mother of three wonderful sons
Adam, Daniel and Jeremy are their names
Dancing and performing was her game
Desdemona was her stage name
Her many styles of dance had won her great fame
Watching her belly dance was ever so neat
Performing at the Renaissance was her gig
Playing with swords and fire would scare you off your feet
One of her joys was teaching others to dance
Sometimes she roped in her mother when she got a chance
Her grandchildren most definitely lit up her life
Kissing and loving them what a delight
She didn't care if you were short or tall
She would go toe to toe with you in a brawl
Her nephews and sons all feared her when she was mad
Because they all knew that they had been bad
When she got upset and on a roll
All of a sudden her mom would get a call
Please, Mom, talk to her and calm her down
Her husband would call out in despair

She was loved by everyone who knew her
Feared by some who had misused her
Her organizational skills were known by all
Her sewing skills were beyond compare
From a simple dress to a beautiful beaded gown
She set up her mannequin and went to town
Her reputation traveled around and around
She had the voice of an Angel
And the wit of Lucille Ball or Carol Burnett
She could keep you in stitches at the drop of a hat
You will always be remembered
With a touch of regret
We lost you much too soon
But your spirit will live on in your kids
Good-bye, Adios from your other mom.

Michelle

She greets you with a warm welcoming smile
Her eyes twinkle when she gives you that smile
Her demeanor is calm and serene
You see when her and her brother were very young they learned
that they were both wheelchair bound
Muscular Dystrophy is the diagnosis they were told
As she grew up she had to watch all the other children at play
Knowing that she couldn't join them and run around
She has to have help to dress and eat
She is making the best of her life and wears it with such grace
The years it took to find such peace.
Why me, dear Lord to have this fate
To be so young and dealing with this disease
Some would have given up when they got the news
She turned to the Lord to help her get through it all
With the Lord by her side she continued to grow
Her loving and nurturing parents were there
holding her hands through it all
She graduated high school and got a college degree
She teaches young children what they need to know
The kids think that she is the cat's meow
She's just their size in her chair, which makes her meet
them eye to eye
To the kids this is oh so neat

Her understanding and compassion make her a great teacher
Even though she has some ongoing health problems,
she doesn't let them get her down
Because of MD she has learned how to be more patient
than other's her age.
We are hoping and praying for a cure to be found
Truly it is a honor to know this beautiful young lady
who walks with God

Mom's Passing

My mother Phyllis always had emphysema and bronchitis from smoking. I was always sure that that when the time came, she would be the first parent I lost. But things got changed and we lost my Dad first. After my father passed, my mother moved into town and rented an apartment.

In the winter of 1985, my sister called and said that Mom's doctor said there was nothing else he could do for her. She had cancer of the lungs and had to have radiation treatments. My mother refused chemotherapy because of all of the side effects. She said she would die before having chemo.

I spent Christmas of 1985 plus January and February of 1986 taking care of my mother. At the end of February, I had to go back to Florida where we had just moved to so I could find a job. My mother spent the last 4 1/2 months of her life in a wonderful nursing home where her mother lived. So every day, her mother got to take care of her daughter until she passed away at 63 years of age.

This time helped my grandmother, who was 85, accept the fact her daughter was dying. It was so hard being away from my mother and knowing that she was going to die. On a Friday in July of 1986, I got a call saying my mother had passed away.

What I learned from the passing of my parents was that life goes on and we all survive. So at the age of 39, I had faced my greatest fear and had lost both of my parents. My security blanket was forever gone. I didn't have time to for a meltdown as I still had three kids at home.

God gives us all the strength we need to go on and survive our greatest fears and losses. My last gift to my mother was my time taking care of her for 2 and 1/2 months before she passed. Thank you, God, for giving me the strength to do this for her.

Mortality

Once we face our own mortality, our life changes
Most of us spend our life fearing death
We fear growing old
In 1999, I faced my own mortality when I was told I had cancer
When my doctor told me I had cancer
and explained my options to me
As I drove home, which was less than ten minutes away,
I made my decision
I told my husband what the doctor told me
and what I was going to have done
Fear never entered my mind as I knew that
God was going to take care of it
I believed that I was going to be fine and
left it in God's hands

That was 20 years ago and I am here writing poems
to read to you from the Lord
From that point on my life has changed,
my priorities about life have changed
What is and isn't important changes
I knew and still know that He has my back
I have become a better person after that

After another traumatic incident, my life changed again
Things I had collected in my life meant nothing anymore
They were just possessions and meant nothing
I became more forgiving because of this incident
You think more about spending time with your loved ones

You realize that we can leave this life at anytime.
We have no guarantees
You learn to appreciate what God has done and
continues to do for us
You realize all you lost was only possessions that can be replaced
What really matters is family that you still have
I have always done things to help people,
still do that and
more for others
Helping others helps to fill my soul,
knowing that this is what the Lord wants us to do
I have a much greater appreciation of life
I was a God fearing Christian before but
some of my priorities were not what He wanted
So he made a drastic change in my life to get me back on track
If you have faced your own mortality,
there is nothing in your future to fear
God is in control and we just need to follow His plan
for us and not our plan for us
Some things in our life we can shake off after they happen
but some things change us forever
They affect our complete future in more ways
than we can imagine
When floods, hurricanes, and other disasters affect people,
I am more compassionate for them
The greatest change has been a closer walk
with the Lord Almighty
I am forever thankful for what He has done to make me a better
person and Christian.
It is never to late to change your life.
All you have to do is want to do it.

My Childhood Perceptions of Growing Up

I grew up in a family of seven. I remember spending a lot of time talking to the elderly people who lived around us. I would go to the grocery store or post office for them. I can't tell you why I did what I did for these people. I was just drawn to do this. For some reason, I felt like I was different, I enjoyed doing things for people but never saw my siblings do this.

I never felt close to my sisters they never seemed to want to be with me, but they were there for each other. I spent a lot of time doing things on my own, because no one wanted to do things with me. So I found ways to occupy myself and not be a nuisance to anyone in my family.

Being a twin means that you are closest to that person. In my life that was not the case. My older sister and I fought all of the time; we couldn't get along and I didn't know why. No one ever said anything about why this was this way or seemed to care. The older I got, the more introverted I became which has affected my whole life.

My sisters are both extroverted so people gravitated to them and I sunk into the background. I was good in a lot of things but never seemed to stand out for them. I wasn't as pretty as my sisters but I did have pretty eyes. My older sister was great in tennis while I was just OK. My sisters had dates and boyfriends and went to the proms. No dates or boyfriends so no prom to go to, that kind of has a sad affect on your self esteem.

From that point on my personality changed and I did what people wanted me to do not necessarily what I wanted to do. When I tried asking people what was going on or writing to them about it didn't get any good response. So getting no answers eventually turned into resentment because I couldn't get answers to things I wanted to know.

Many years later, when I finally got some answers, I found some peace and stopped letting these things bother me so much, the pain went away. But I was quite old before this finally happened but I'm glad it did.

If you can find other people who had childhoods like you did, it will help you all overcome a lot of the issues and bad feelings that you have about your past. Just be aware that no matter what happened in your childhood was not because of anything you did but more lack of understanding all around.

Just by understanding more it will help you start the healing process that you need. Having answers allows you to stop living for their love and approval in your life. You can learn to accept what they have to offer and learn to be content with that. This will allow you to find inner peace and tranquility in your life. It is so hard to live never getting the love and acceptance that we all crave in our life.

As children, we expect people to love and care for us when that doesn't happen it changes us totally as a person. We grow up being someone different than what we were supposed to be.

Until we can understand our childhood, we cannot move on to our adulthood. Being able to understand your childhood will be a major breakthrough in dealing with everything else in our lives.

I am hoping that by writing this that it will help people to understand their life. If it happened to you, my hope is that you can learn and get past all the pain and anger.

If you are the parent of a child going through this, try to develop a new relationship with them so their future can change. If you see this happening to some child, try to get them to talk to you or let them read this story in the hope that it will help them to understand.

The most important thing is to keep believing in God as he is always there with you. Talk to your guardian angel and tell her what you need in order to improve your life. You are never alone in your life reach out to family and friends to help. Whatever hand you have been dealt in your life always try to live it so that God would be proud of you and you can walk with your head held high.

Thank you, Lord, for always watching over, caring for and loving me. Praise the Lord.

My Younger Brother

This is the one that nearly destroyed me. I spent three weeks out of every month taking care of my brother at the nursing home he was in, When he was 53, his blood sugar was going out of control, which led to his renal failure. His renal failure led to his being put on a medical flight to a bigger hospital. He developed blood poisoning and had to have his leg amputated to the knee, and also had to have kidney dialysis for a short time.

Since riding his Harley was his life, he gave up and just wanted to die. He went from weighing 200 pounds down to 80 pounds when he passed. My brother and I were very close. I would stay at his house when I came home. Bob was a correction officer and loved his job. My brother passed away four days after his 54th birthday and that was 11 years ago. He is forever loved and forever missed.

My baby brother was nine years younger than me. When I married and came home with my kids, Bob was 11 or 12 years old so he helped me look after the kids. My husband and I were stationed in Germany when my brother got married. Before our tour was over three years later, I received a phone call saying my brother and his wife had been in a bad car accident. His pregnant wife died a couple of days after the accident. My brother was still in the hospital when his wife and child were buried.

From that point, on he lost his will to live, so he drank a lot, drove his car and Harley real fast. When he was diagnosed as a diabetic, he didn't take care of himself. He wanted to die but would not kill himself because we had already lost our parents and a brother so there was just the four of us left.

Besides being a correction officer at a prison, my brother taught Taekwondo for 30 years and was a fifth-degree black belt, which made him quite respected in his hometown. But losing the love of his life, took everything out of his life. This is still a hard loss to bear. See you in heaven, Bob.

No Intimacy. What Now?

No one to hold
A love gone cold
Questions never answered
Or am I deaf
No emotions shown
My heart seems so dead
Special dates don't seem to matter
No cards given for the latter
Please don't do this I often say
Seems to fall on deaf ears
Doesn't matter what I say
Always do things your own way
So I guess I'll stop and be quiet
Before I explode and create a riot
Love that used to burn so bright
Will hardly show any light
Pain keeps growing everyday
Hoping for solutions as you pray
Have prayed so long and nothing changes
Like a bad book you reject the pages
Hoping for a happy ending
Not seeing signs so nothings pending
Totally relying on the Lord above
To light a fire under the one I love
To rekindle the flame that seems to be gone
Praying for a miracle all day long
Until that time comes, please, Lord,
keep me surrounded by your love.

Nurses

When God created the people who would become nurses, he added a extra big dose of compassion. Most of the nurses I have met in my hospital stays go the extra mile to make your stay special.

They have the never-ending gift of patience. They don't snap or put you down, when you are in extreme pain or cannot do some task shortly after surgery.

They remind me of my grandma who was a nurse; she could always make things ok. No matter how bad it was, my grandma could fix anything.

Either with special grandma kisses on your booboo. Or maybe just giving you a big hug till you stopped crying. Maybe a secret cookie to make it all well.

These special people go the extra mile to help soothe your pain whether physical or emotional. They know the special words to tell you when you need them. They take the time to answer your prayers and just talk to you. They will explain whatever you want to know. If you are the parent of a patient, they will explain what the doctor did and why he did it. They will build up our spirits when our loved ones are having hard times. They know what we are going through and what reassurance we need to hear to put us at peace. They have the little extra bits of information that the doctor doesn't tell us.

Nurses calm all of our fears and worries. She is the missing link between our surgery and our complete recovery. They know that we need a little TLC from time to time and are happy to provide it. The really good nurses are the ones who make your stay enjoyable and try to keep you as pain free as possible.

Most of the time you will know who these extra special ones are by just talking to them. You see in their demeanor the love they have for the job they do. Sometimes they are that shoulder to cry on when someone you love has just passed away. At other times they are the ones that you can laugh with over the goofiest things. Their jobs most of the time involve dealing with life and death. When needed, the comfort they offer and give us is the only thing that keeps us going. When the news is just the opposite, they are the ones who are jumping with joy when we get to go home.

Even though they have hard jobs, they try not to let us see how their jobs affect them. Instead, they put on a cheerful smile and start a new day.

Thank you for being God's angels in the hospital when we need them most.

May God Bless all of you wonderful people.

Obedience

God wants to know where your obedience lies.
Is it with Him and His word?
Is it with your parents?
Is it with a bottle of booze?
Is it in doing sinful things that God abhors?
If it is with your parents and you are a child,
that is where God wants it to be.
Listen to them and learn from them about Him
Let them teach you about right and wrong.
Let them teach you about Me.
That will please Me so much.
If it is with a bottle of booze or drugs, then I am not pleased.
I ask you to turn to me and My Word for help.
Pray to Me and ask Me for guidance and for help to defeat the
Devil who is tempting you to this way of life.
Ask Me to cure you of your terrible addiction
whether it be drugs or booze

Are you breaking one of God's commandments?
Ask God to help you find answers to the
many questions that you have
Pray to Him to strengthen you and to lead you
back to the road that leads to Him
Pray for His forgiveness in having strayed away
from His teachings

Is it your friends who are constantly trying to get you
to forget His words and do things that you know are wrong?

Most of all, don't let the devil have any say
or influence in your life
If he tries, tell him you are God's child and to get lost
He is the path to life everlasting
He is the one who can restore peace and faith back in your life
He is the one who created you and
has loved you since the day you were born
He is the one who defeated the Devil and banished him to hell

When things seem to be going wrong in your life,
please reach out your hand to Me
and ask for My healing love to enter your life

God cries for us when He sees us in situations or life styles
that He knows are not His plan for us
Sit down and ponder all the things or areas
in your life where you have strayed from Him
Please be honest with yourself as you are the only one
who can honestly answer this
Once you see there are things in your life that need correcting,
get on your knees and pray to Him for forgiveness, courage, and
the wisdom and clarity to help you change your life.
Just ask, as He is only a prayer away.

God loves you and is always there to help you.
Amen.
Thank you, God.

One of Two

Have you ever stopped to think what being a twin was like? Your life is always shared with someone. Your birthday and your graduation too.

The pros are you always have a playmate to play with and talk to. At times, you can also have a partner in crime to do things with. If you want to play hopscotch, jacks, and such you have someone to play with.

The cons are you never have your own birthday cake. The celebration is always shared with someone else. If they are more outgoing and prettier than you, you deal with them being popular and you not being popular. They get dates and go to proms and you sit at home wishing things were different. Hoping someday that you would have a boyfriend also. My twin was an extrovert and made friends very easily, I was a shy introvert who did not make friends easily. Once you get to know me my true self comes out but until that time, I will be quiet as a mouse.

We were about the same height and weight, I was a couple of inches taller than her. We were both very athletically inclined, which seemed to run in our family. I was right-handed with brown eyes and she was left-handed with blue eyes. I have had to wear glasses from the age of 9 months until today; before that my sight was just shadows and blurs. She needed glasses much later in life.

Since my mother did not know she was carrying twins, the amount of calcium was drastically depleted. I was constantly seeing the dentist because of the lack of calcium, having cavities repaired. Even having had fluoride treatments given to us, I had to have full dentures by the time I was in my middle twenties.

She still has all her own teeth to this day. She would get in trouble for throwing my glasses down the basement stairs.

When I was 16, I got contact lenses and wore them success-fully for 20 years. But due to getting corneal abrasions, I stopped wearing them later in life.

For some reason, I never understood we were never as close as I thought that twins should be. We played together sometimes when we were younger. But most of the time we each went our separate ways. This was more apparent when we got older. We had different friends and different hobbies.

We both babysat and detasseled corn in the summer. We both had paper routes in our town. She had the route that was closest to our house. I had the route on the other side of the tracks that went out to the highway and was several blocks longer than hers. One Christmas, I almost got frostbite, it was so cold, and one year she got bitten by a dog on her route.

We lived in a small rural town, so we had lots of play spaces. The neighbor's side yard was our baseball diamond, the other neighbor's yard was our croquette playing area. The streets were our tennis courts until a car was coming.

Until we were 18, our birthday cakes were shared. Three years later, I had a daughter born the day before my birthday, so once again I was sharing my birthday. My twin sister is very close in heart even though we live very far apart.

Pastor Roger

You heard the Lord a calling, laying in a field where you had fallen. The wonder of His words as He talked to you. From that day forward, He couldn't forget what the Lord had said to him.

So off to be a pastor is what became of him. From that day on you were hooked, the Holy Bible was your book.

You found a beautiful woman who believed like you, and was more than happy to begin this walk with you. After you got married, living in God's word you would tarry.

Through the good times, and the bad, through the happy times and the sad. Thru the ups and downs your Bible was always around. You raised your children in God's ways. Teaching them the 10 Commandments and the Golden Rule, they grew up to be your pride and joy.

You moved from church to church but then you found your own special church. It's called Grace Church and its in a small town, with lots of pastures and farm land around. You preached so well it started to grow, a bigger place you needed to go. You found a bigger place and fixed it up, now many years later it is no longer enough. A bigger place is needed again. What a tribute to your vision and a gift of God's grace.

Roger, you taught us how we should be, when that wasn't what we wanted to be. You taught us what the Lord wanted us to know and do. You taught us to do God's will as we struggled up life's many hills.

Roger was the kind of man we all want as a friend, always there with a helping hand. In times of need he was there to listen and give a little advice. Maybe just a big hug and a scripture or two.

He touched most of our lives at some point in time. He will always be remembered as one of a kind. He walked the Lord's walk and talked the Lord's talk. He was kind, compassionate, loving, patient, and forgiving. He showed us that the Lord forgives us no matter what we do.

Our church and our town were honored to have had Roger Olsen as part of our community. Enjoy your mansion, Roger, you deserve it. You will be missed by everyone for a long time to come.

People Who Pay It Forward

Many people have lived their whole lives doing good things for others and expecting nothing in return. They never told anyone NO. They are the type of people who would give you the last shirt off of their back. I don't think that the word No exist in their vocabulary. Their heart goes out to anyone who is undergoing anything, illness, loss of property etc. They are the first ones to help or to ask if the other person needed anything. It is just an automatic gesture on their part, it is never a conscientious thought.

Most of their lives these people are caregivers, they take care of others and are always there for others. They never think about their own wants and needs they are solely concerned with others. This trait probably started showing itself when they were a small child. They were out helping older citizens do yard work or running errands for them. They do various types of deeds some are very small so no one even knows they did it. A few things are really big and involve a lot of people to help them complete it. They have a compassionate and giving nature.

Helping people happens at church, at work, at home or anywhere the need arises. I'm guessing many of you are thinking of some people that you know who are like that. It may be an aunt, uncle, mom, dad, sister, brother, cousin or a neighbor or a good friend. Most of the time people seem to like them and some people pick up on the fact that they like to help others. Some people have experienced a lot of tragedies in their life and others have experienced very little in there's.

Giving and doing for others comes as natural to them as breathing comes to us all. What they do is an automatic reflex to a certain situation. What they do they do out of the goodness of there heart, It is done to nourish there souls and for no other reason. They do it because it is the right thing to do, it is what God wants them to do. They are a good example of their faith. Doing good for our neighbors like the Lord tells us to do, love one another. If you know someone like this, you may also realize that it is really hard for them to accept help when they need it. Even if something major happens in their lives they will blow it off as no big deal. They do not think that what they do is anything special, so expecting help in return isn't expected.

Getting someone like this to accept any help is tricky, you have to remind them of all the good that they have done for others. Then tell them that this is pay back for all that they have done. They will accept the help because it was offered in the proper spirit of giving. Doing what the Lord wants, do unto others as you would have others do unto you. For people who are new to religion, that is known as The Golden Rule. Thank you Lord for giving us hearts and souls that want to give.

Perseverance

As I was growing up and many things happened, I used to refer to them as tests.

Now I know that it was God testing my perseverance. Would I accept the challenge or give up?

My first test was when Jerry, my older brother and protector, was killed in a car accident. I was 16 years old at the time. I felt so all alone because he was my protector. Between God and my Guardian Angel, I made it through that time.

Before I turned 40 years old, my greatest fear came true. My father fell ill and passed away within a week of being diagnosed. Three years later, my mother was diagnosed with cancer. I spent two and a half months taking care of her and four months later, she passed away. Being a wife and mother didn't allow me time to just give up. I persevered through this with God's help and guidance.

My parents never got to see my children grow up and get married. They never got to meet their great-grandkids and see them grow up and get married. They never got to know their nine great-great-grandchildren. They missed out on those memories. Losing my parents at such a young age was so very hard to bear. Also losing them so close together was really hard.

All was well for ten years. Then I was diagnosed with breast cancer. I gave it to the Lord to handle and He brought me through it. That was 21 years ago.

Four years later, my husband had to have quadruple bypass heart surgery. But he had just had knee replacement so he went home on heart therapy medicine and three months later, he had his heart surgery. Another job for me to persevere through; by that time, our children were grown and lived far away. So the Lord helped me to get through this six months of recovery and take care of him and continue to work at the same time.

In 2009, I spent eight months taking care of my baby brother, who was dying from complications of diabetes. His passing took me years to deal with.

I figured God was not done with me yet, so I keep going waiting for the next test. In 2012, my mother-in-law passed away from a stroke. We stepped up to spend time helping my father-in-law with whatever he needed to do.

In 2013, my brother-in-law Gary passed away in his sleep. I spent the next several years supporting my sister-in-law. In 2014, we moved in with my father-in-law to help take care of him; he was 89. In 2017, I had to have bypass heart surgery for myself and two months later, my twin sister's husband passed away from an auto-immune disease. In 2018, my best childhood friend, Sheryne, I grew up with, passed away.

The next, day my favorite cat Darcie passed away one day after my friend's passing. Three months later, my father-in-law, who was 93, passed away from congestive heart disease.

So the Lord was having a busy time with me and supporting me through all that had to be done after that. I'm sitting here waiting for the next test.

Thank you, God for always being there, holding me and supporting me through all of these tests.

Power of Praise

Having been raised in a religion where the Bible was not read, I attended a church where it was read. This intrigued me.

In 1998, we started attending a church where reading the Bible was highly encouraged. We joined a Bible study group, the nice things was one of the people in this group loved reading the history of the Bible. When he talked of the Bible, he could tell you what was going on in history at that time also. So he made learning the Bible interesting.

As I continued to read the Bible I was slowly learning more and more about God and Jesus. Then we moved to Oklahoma and I became very good friends with the new temporary pastor and his wife at the church we were attending. She and her husband were very helpful to me. We figured God had put us both in the same place at the same time to help each other, that friendship lasted till she died four years ago. Her husband and I still call and check on each other from time to time. Later we moved back to Wisconsin to be here to help his aging parents.

I have always tried to thank God every night for all of the blessings He gives us each day. But until recently after reading *Prison to Praise,* I finally know that He wants us also to praise and thank Him for all of the good and bad things in my life. The more I read and learn, I begin to understand how important praising Him is in our lives. Things may be good or so we think but they can also be better. By praising Him, we bless and enrich our own lives. We learn that things happen through him, we need to praise him when the devil starts filling us with falsehoods.

By praising Him all the time, when normally we would do or say something or get mad defeats Him. The more we praise Him, the more things in our lives start to change for the better. Our lives will also greatly change due to these changes, it will come slowly sometimes and other times the changes will be fast.

I know that I would never ever have thought about thanking God for the hard and hurtful things that happened in my life until I read that book. But it makes sense since all things come through Him who made all things. So don't get upset anymore. Just praise the Lord instead.

Praise

Pouring out our hearts to the Lord
Remembering everything that He does for us
because He loves us
Allowing Him to be the guiding light in our lives
Inspiring us to reach out to others
and tell them about the Lord
Singing songs in glory of how wonderful He is
Endearing our spirits to always walk with Him.

Praise to You

I can't count the number of times I let You down
Or count the times I disappointed You
The times I did wrong knowing it wasn't right
The people I hurt
The ones I disappointed and let down
But I can't find a time when You let me down
You are always there no matter what I do
You take me back as if I have never done anything wrong
You only see the good in me
You do your best to build me up when I'm going astray
You are always there guarding my back
I am eternally grateful that You care so much for me
My praise of You can never be enough to cover everything
that You have done for me
That You continue to do every day in my life
I am grateful for all the gifts You have given me
May I always be a warrior with words to say the things
You want me to say
You are my light, my love, and my Savior
I thank You with every breath I take.

Published in *Best Poets of 2019*

Present Christmas Feelings

Now 40 years later and the fun is all gone
I do all the traditional things
Send out Christmas cards
Buy presents for those I love
Christmas day is nothing special
because there is no family here
My parents have both passed on
My grandmother and my aunt also are gone
Both of my brothers are no longer here
I have one aunt that is still here
My children are all grown with children of their own
Most of my grandchildren are grown
with children of their own
My great-grandchildren are still young
My children all live in different states
Coming home for Christmas doesn't work
So since so many relatives have all passed away
There is no big get together for my family
I'm so alone
My husband's parents are both gone
His middle brother is also gone
He has a younger one who is still here
So no big gatherings with family and friends
So one of my favorite times has come to be one of the worst
No family to love and be with without traveling so far

No children and their family's coming home
I hate feeling so all alone
'Cause it just feels like any other day
Nothing to look forward to. be grateful
to have family with you
Just so thankful that Jesus was born on that day
Gives me something to be happy about on Christmas Day

Reaching Out

Normally reaching out means extending our hand or arm to enable us to pick up something But the one that I am going to write about is reaching out of ourselves to do what the Lord wants us to do.

Most people are most comfortable in their own little space whether that is their home or just a room in their home.

What we need to do is to learn how to reach out as our Heavenly Father desires us to do. Our Lord wants us to reach out and help people in whatever way we can. Seeing what a person might need even if they don't say a word. For instance, looking at someone and seeing the pain in them even if they don't say a word. Going up to them and asking if it is OK with them to give them a hug from the Lord because He sees their pain. Or maybe just asking if they need to talk to someone about something that is bothering them.

Being able to step outside of our own comfort zone, We are not generally comfortable doing something for a complete stranger. We are OK doing this for people we know like family and someone who lives in our neighborhood.

But just stepping out and doing something for a stranger is what the Lord wants us to do. This is where the saying Love one another enters into our life, doing things for others because it is the right thing to do. If you see someone having a financial hardship and you can give them some money to help, do it. Because if the situation was reversed you would appreciate getting some money when you are feeling so helpless and desperate. Maybe they lost their job and need groceries or need to pay there electric bill.

Maybe volunteering somewhere is more of what you are comfortable doing, go for it. Doing something like this will help someone who needs the help as well as fill a need in your soul. Go through your house and find things you no longer want or need and find someone who could use these things. But best of all you can just give them to someone. You get to clean out space and they get things that they need. To me it is just such a good feeling helping others just because we can.

Or maybe you are more comfortable reaching out to people and sharing God's word with them. Showing them all of the things the Lord can and will do for them if they just ask earnestly. The Lord loves it when we ask to help others not ourselves. Some people are too proud to ask for help, so having help given without them having to ask or beg for it is a blessing. Handing out Bibles to people who have never read one before. These are things that the Lord desires us to do. He wants us to reach out and grow in our religion. He wants us to grow as children of God. He wants us to know that asking for His help is what he is waiting for. Just the simplest act of friendship has far-reaching effects you may never see.

Robin and Herman

To the newlyweds, Robin and Herman
Blessings for the both of you
Two people who walk hand and hand with the Lord
Leading the way showing others how to follow the lord
You both lead by example in your lives
Your lives have been a steady journey with the Lord
Robin, your love for children is plain for all to see
Teaching God's children all the things
He wants them to learn
Herman, you have led so many young and old to the Lord
You both have suffered a loss but the Lord has led you to
happiness again
May you as a couple continue to be strong leaders
in and outside of the church
God has blessed you both with a new love and a new partner
May the years ahead be filled with wonderful memories and
lots of new experiences together
God brought you two together so He has great plans for you
Wishing you many, many years of great joy and love

April 6, 2019
Sharron Dorst

Russell

He was what people called "one in a million." He had so much charisma, like my brother Bob, they could sell you anything before you even knew it. And as you were walking away scratching your head trying to figure out how you were going to explain what just happened. He was an absolutely charming persn, who could relate to everyone.

If you called him your friend, that bond was forever. I am so proud to have been his friend.

His love of family and friends was endless, there was nothing that he wouldn't do or couldn't do for these people.

He struggles with losing his dad, which changed his future. He moved back home to be there to help and support his mother in the future.

He was one of those people who would give you the shirt off his back if you needed it. His kindness was endless. As much as we all loved him and will miss him, God had a special job that only Russell could fill.

God, bless him until we meet up again. What a party that will be!

Sandy

I remember seeing you walking around with a smile on your face. Greeting people and talking to them when they came to church. You had a lot to carry working a full-time job, as well as being the pastor's wife. Meetings for work, meeting for the church, fixing supper and cleaning the house. I will never know how you did it all and still had time for lunches with friends. You had women's group meetings once a month, synergy meetings twice a month, and many others things you needed to do.

Your smile was always so genuine to see. Your compassion and love were there for all to see. I can't imagine all of the many people that you have prayed for over the years. Couples that you have counseled through their worries and fears. Youngsters you have taught lessons about God in the classroom. You are a wonderful grandmother, showing those kids God's love and ways.

You are a powerful speaker when you are asked to speak. Your knowledge of the Bible is what makes your advice so dear. Getting to know you over the years has been a treat. You make people feel like they are important. That whatever they say you are eager to hear. You bring a smile to peoples faces when you talk to them. Just getting a hug from you can cheer someone up. Too many people can see someone in pain and walk on by. But your compassion demands that you go over to them and say something or just give them a hug. God's guiding hand and love radiates from you. People are drawn to you for that reason, you let people see what the Lord has done in you. His word and teachings freely flow from you.

You have raised wonderful children who love you and reflect your walk with the Lord. You showed them by example what their walk with the Lord should look like. Seeing the peace on your face makes me want to know you much better. That kind of peace is what we all want in our lives. I know that the Lord is always going to be walking with you no matter what you do. All of the women that you have befriended will always sing your praises. They are molding their lives to be more like you.

God bless you. God is smiling so brightly when He thinks of you. He will say to you, "Thank you, my good and faithful servant."

Save Us from Politicians

The bane of our existence, who hold our future in their hands. They tell us they will do this and that if they are elected, but all of it are lies. They are going to do whatever they want to make money for themselves with no thought to the people they represent. It is all about what special interest groups want to get done.

I bet the Lord would have a really hard time trying to find ten honest, moral, God-fearing people among them all. Our forefathers were all God-fearing and all of their decisions were made for the betterment of our country. Everything they did, they did for us, not for themselves. Why can't we have people like that in office now? Our forefathers must be rolling over in their graves over the poor decisions and corruption in our government.

So Lord, you need to step in and clean up our government, to be what you want it to be again. We the people need Your help. We are thankful that You are always here watching over and protecting us. Please, Lord save us.

Second Chances
JoDee and Scott on February 28, 2015

You each will marry the love of your life
Did you ever think the day you met
This would be the person you would wed
The long road back to trust and love
Having each of them thrown away like a rug
The courage it takes to start dating anew
Opening up your heart to feeling again
Scott has such caring and giving ways
His protective nature makes JoDee feel so loved
His kindness and gentleness is so plain to see
JoDee has had many heartbreaks in her life
Your joy for living shines from your eyes
Her loving and giving spirit is clear for all to see
The start of a wonderful new beginning
With the person you lovingly adore
Sharing the good times as well as the sad times
Always keep the road to communication open
Always show the one you love how much they are loved
Being equal partners will ensure your marriage will last
Work as hard at marriage as you do at your job
Never take each other for granted
If you have an argument or fight
Stop and think of all of the reasons you love each other
Always make up before its bedtime
May God always be there to bless and keep you both

Seeking God

We spend a lot of our life looking for
and seeking acceptance from others
We do it in our marriage
wanting acceptance from our spouse
We seek acceptance from our family and friends
We need acceptance at our job site from our co-workers
Sometimes we even want it from a stranger
Mostly we seek it from our church
Being accepted or approved of is part of our DNA
This has always been a part of our life
But can we honestly say that we give our all in seeking and ac-
cepting God's will for our lives
Do we seek His approval for the things we do
or have done in and with our lives
Accepting God's will in all phases of our life
not just certain areas
God's greatest wish is for us to accept
and seek Him in our lives
When we accept God in our lives,
we have someone else walking with us
When we accept God's love for us,
we know He has our back
Our lives seem much easier when we accept the Lord
Even in our darkest times, He is always there for us
We need to make it a daily job to seek out the Lord
We may seek Him but most of the time,
it is only occasionally we do it

Most of the time is when we are in some troubling situation
Or when we have lost someone very close to us
We need to always be seeking a closer walk with Him
Do this with every fiber in your body
Don't do this passively but as aggressively as possible
In today's world, we cannot afford not to do this
If we fail in seeking Him, we are the ones who will suffer
The cost of not having Him in our lives
is something I don't think any of us wish to pay
So pray to and praise Him all you can

Sheryne

It doesn't seem like a year has passed.
Some days went fast and others seemed to last
I miss our calls, hearing your voice and
spending time with you at your beautiful house
Your many, many friends miss hearing from you
Your funeral service was beautiful and
Alex's song left not a dry eye in the room
Standing room only in the room,
but longer lines waiting to get into the building
Pink was oh so sad but Raoul stepped up
and took your place
Pink is so spoiled, pampered and loved
Someday she will join you in the heavens above
Your family and I all miss and love you so much
Your little fenced-in plot with your flowers is a joy to see,
done by Raoul who so loved thee
Till we see you again face to face

Sixty Years Ago

God said a special blessing the day you two were wed. He asked that you would have a family someday. He also blessed you both with kind hearts, loving personalities, and compassion for others. His special blessing has served you well for all of these years.
You both are warm and open to everyone you meet. The way that you treat others is always done with God's grace.

You make people feel that your really do care and that you are so happy that they are there. There is nothing fake or put on in your life; what people see in you is what your really are. I have always admired the style and grace that you carry with you. The love you show your family always brings a smile to my face.

You have four beautiful children who you are so proud of. Looking at them is like looking in a mirror of your endless love. They are perfect reflections of their parents' patience, love, compassion, and their belief in God up above.

Every once in a while, you meet a couple who just seems to have it all. The love and respect that people have for each other. The unending love that is still alive after all of this time. The respect from others who know them well. You both are such great role models for future generations to aspire to be. May God continue to share His blessing in the rest of your life. To two wonderful, generous, loving, and compassionate people we all want to be when we grow up.

Happy 60th Anniversary, Bob and Shelby!

Sleepless Nights

I have a lot of sleepless nights. Either I lie down and can't sleep or I go to sleep and several hours later, wake up and can't go back to sleep. Either way, I get up and play games on my tablet or I sit down and write something.

I feel like everything that I write is God inspired. He gives me the thoughts and words to write. Like I have told others, if it is something that I am meant to write about it, will be done in 15 minutes. If it is not meant for me to write about it at this time, I can sit there for days and the words won't come. People who write novels or columns for the newspaper know this feeling. But they also know that when the words don't come, it is called writer's block.

So I'm guessing that my sleepless nights are God's way of talking to me and getting me ready to write. Once I sit down and write one or two things, then I can go back to bed and sleep. I'm thinking these nights are God's way of communicating with me. In my sleep, He puts these thoughts and ideas in my head.

God is so inspirational in what He can and does teach us. If God wants to me to write it, He will nag at me till I do His will. He is always the loving, positive one who pushes me to do things. I'm the Doubting Thomas who says why would anyone want to read something that I wrote.

I need to realign my thinking, if it is what God wants said, it must be important in some way. So I have learned over the years it is just easier to sit down and do as He wishes. He has the grand plan and I am just the instrument He is using to say these things.

Don't ever think that just because you don't have a college degree or know the Bible from cover to cover, you can't do this.

God uses people for many reasons. Maybe you have grown up in an abusive household and need to tell others there's hope. Maybe you used drugs and alcohol for many years and stopped; your story may be the inspirational story for someone else to stop doing drugs. You can be the catalyst who shows them that there is hope. They can change their life; all they have to do is really want it.

Reading about someone's near-death experience shows us that God does exist and shows us that our faith in the Lord is justified. If He can die on the cross and three days later arise and go home to His Father, there is nothing that He cannot do. Imagine what He can and will do in your life if you just believe in Him. With the Lord on our side, there isn't anything we can't do. Just believe He has your back and He will guide you.

Our faith and belief in Him is our pearl in our oyster. We have hit the jackpot and don't even know it. With the Lord at our back, anything is possible. We just need to have the confidence to get it done. We don't know the relevance of what we are doing but He does. Thank you, Lord, for believing in me. Praise Your name.

Small-Town Living

I grew up in a very small town under 500 people, and most of them lived in the country.

I had an older brother and sister and my twin sister and me. Four kids, two newborns, a two-year-old and a four-year-old. I don't know how my parents did it but they did.

Our little group had two sides when we fought: my brother and me, and my two sisters together. The sides came into play when my twin sister and I would have a fight. If I hit her, she would tell my older sister, who would then hit me. Then I would tell my older brother, who would then hit my older sister, or it would be reversed if she hit me. We were very protective of each other,thus the sides, so we grew up always having one of our older siblings covering our back.

Older kids were weary of picking on us because of our older siblings. My brother was the leader of the pack and we all fell under him. My older sister and my twin were extroverts and outgoing; they easily made friends. I on the other hand was, and still am, an introvert, which makes it very hard for me to reach out to new people. When I make friends, they are lifetime ones until they break my trust. It is so very hard for me to forgive them. But the old saying that some people are in your life for a reason or season or for all time.

My sisters and I were not close as children so I spent a lot of my time alone and doing things by myself. I spent a great deal of time talking to the older people who lived around us, helping them in any way I could whether cleaning their yards or going to the post office or getting groceries for them. I visited and talked to a neighbor who had lost his legs in a car accident.

We used to play baseball in our neighbor's side yard, which was big. We played croquet in another neighbor's front yard. We had free rein to go anywhere in our small town. It was safe and everybody knew who we were, where we lived, and who our parents were. So needless to say, if you did anything you should not be doing, our parents knew about it before we got home. So getting away with anything was totally impossible. So when you were asked if anything happened today, you'd better tell the truth because they already knew; if you lied the punishment was worse because you lied.

We had sidewalks on which to play jacks and hopscotch on. We had second-hands bikes our dad fixed up for us. I guess we were considered poor but we never felt that way. We always had food on the table and clothes and shoes to wear, even though they were second-hand. We had a house with a big yard to play in so we felt rich. When we got older, we played tennis in the street, which was only four blocks long. We could see when cars turned on the street and have plenty of time to get off before they reached us. If we wanted a real baseball game, we could go to the school grounds and play there.

When we were in second grade, they built a new school where we went until we graduated. All four of us kids were very athletic; we played tennis, tag, baseball, and touch football. When we got to high school, we all participated in a lot of sports and school activities. My brother was the jock playing baseball, football, basketball, and he participated in track. My older sister was very good in tennis and loved to play golf. My twin sister and I played tennis and girls' basketball.

In the summer, we dug up part of the backyard so we could grow a garden. So we had to dig it up, rake it, plant all of the seeds and weed it. Also in the summer, we girls would detassel corn, the perfect job—you could get a suntan and be able to flirt with the boys. My brother would work pulling out the weeds for the farmers who grew beans. We used the money we made doing those jobs to buy our school clothes so our mom and dad only had to buy our school supplies.

By then we had another brother so buying for five kids was a lot. When our baby brother was due for shots, we all went with our mom to the doctor's office After he had his shots and was crying, we grabbed him and walked out of the doctor's office, giving the doc a dirty look. The doctor looked at my mother and said, "If you offend one, I guess you offend them all."

She said, "Yes, you do."

My older sister and I fought the whole time we were growing up, so it was fun when we all shared a room. My twin sister had the single bed and my older sister and I had the bunk beds. If we were fighting, I would bounce her bunk until she threatened to pee on me if I didn't stop. Usually she and I would be outside fist fighting in the side yard. That was our life until our older brother was killed in a car accident while on leave from the Marine Corps. I lost my protector and life wasn't the same anymore. Those years were really hard on me because I felt all alone.

After I graduated from high school, I left home and a year later got married and started having my children. When I went home, my baby brother, who was nine years younger than I was, would help watch the kids. We became good friends through those years, so I felt I had a protector again.

We were best of friends until he died at age 54. I cared for him for eight months when he was dying, because we had already lost our parents many years before that.

It took a lot of time for us girls to come together and forgive our past fighting. We now plan a sister trip every year. One sister plans the whole trip and the next year another sister gets to do it. We have seen a lot of country and different places and had a lot of fun.We have also learned about each other as parents and sisters. We have a great respect for each other as the three of us are all that's left of our family. We have been doing this for 20 years and can't wait for the next one.

The message of this whole story is that life is too short. If you have family separation, mend it before it is too late and they are gone. There is nothing that I wouldn't give to have all of my family here with me.

Don't live your life with regrets because of all the things you should or could have done.

Synergy

The coming together or merging of things, thoughts and ideas for a greater good.

Our years coming together for Synergy. People have shared their time, beliefs, visions and messages from God. Opening ourselves to what others have to say. Hearing your messages from others, sharing how they impacted their lives. All of us giving our time to come spend it with the Lord. Sharing time out of our busy lives to opening our minds to hear what you have to say. To hear peoples prayers and send your healing blessing to us whether physical, emotional or spiritual where healing is needed.

For allowing people to see, hear and feel your spirit surrounding us. For freeing us of our problems, health issues, marriage conflicts, feelings of loneliness that we all have felt at some point in our lives. For helping us to realize that we are not alone in life. We have you for guidance, all we have to do is ask for your help. We learn that a lot of other people are suffering or have suffered the same thing. Let us always raise our voices in praise to you, Showing you with our voices what you mean to us.

Thank you for giving us prayers teams to pray over us and pass on your thoughts to us. For placing healing hands on us to ease our suffering, and to lift up our spirits when we are feeling down and in need of your love.

For refreshing our hearts, our spirits and our souls with your words. For always allowing us to share with you and others how you have been there to help us. Hearing from others helps us to grow more and more in our faith.

I wish more and more people would come to Synergy and see what it could do for them. Thank you for inspiring our church to start Synergy at our church. I'm sure that many people have received healing, inspiration and freedom from the many burdens that they have carried. Thank you, Lord

Taking God's Greatness for Granted

Last week, while driving through the Rocky Mountains, I was in awe at His work. The huge mountains and peaks that He created. The various color and size of these mountains. The huge canyons that He created there. The water running through them. Seeing snow at the top of some of those mountains.

In California, there are a lot of brown shrubs and desert-like scenery, hardly any green like we take for granted back here in Wisconsin.

In Utah, the Great Salt Flats stretch for miles. In Nebraska, there is mile after mile of flat land. Out east and west, there is so much land and many open spaces to see, as well as stunning waterfalls, rivers, and streams to see. Beautiful sunsets wherever you may be.

Here there are deer, elk, ducks, and turkeys that hunters love to hunt. The fertile fields to grow food for humans and feed for farm animals.

The states that are warm most of the time and the different produce they grow there. But over time, I have seen a lot of water sources drying up. There are drought conditions in many states and water restrictions in others.

Please be aware of these things before they are gone. God has given us all of theses things and we have stopped appreciating them. As in our lives, we take all of this for granted, not thanking Him all of the time for this beautiful world that He has given us. Slow down and look at His work. Close your eyes and hear His work. Sit down at the dining room table and enjoy the meal from His work. Seeing all of this amazes me and leaves me in wonder of our Lord. If this was all done in seven days, I can't wait to see heaven and everything He has waiting for us.

This world leaves me in awe but I imagine that Eternity will leave me speechless. So please stop taking His work for granted. Thank you, Lord, for all of your wonders.

The Four Seasons

Spring—when flowers are starting to bloom. That is like little children who are old enough to know about God, watching them blossom as they learn about the Lord. Learning about all the things the Lord has made for us. We see the light starting to shine in their eyes as they learn more and more. Like fertilizer makes the flowers grow, God's love and His words teach them how the Lord wants them to grow.

Summertime—when things are growing and producing. In our summertime, we are going from childhood to adulthood. God has fertilized and nurtured the seeds that were planted in the spring. Are we going to continue following the Lord through His word or are we going to cause it to rain? We need to stop and rethink if we are drifting from His path. Light sprinkles will slow us down, but lightning and thunder can stop us in our tracks. Summer is a time to grow and become stronger.

Fall is like middle age. We are older and figure we know it all. But like the falling leaves, we learn about all the areas we still need to work on. Sometimes like all the falling leaves or natural disasters, we hit a brick wall. The mess we have made in our lives brings us to our knees. Cleaning up is a slow and sometimes painful process. But the glory of the Lord is there waiting for us.

Winter is a long cold time for some of us. It is kind of like becoming a senior citizen reminding us of all the good and bad things in our lives. There may be hard times yet to come. But like all things through God, the sun will shine. It gives us time to reflect on our lives. To examine areas that we may need to fix while we have the time. But once we get through all the snow and ice, we know that spring will come and make all things grow again. Our lives are just like the four seasons from a newborn child to hopefully eternity. Praise the Lord.

The Green Door Gang

The Green Door Gang is a group of older people who enjoy having fun and meeting new people. There is always a lot of things for younger people to do, but no one thinks about what we would like to do. Sure we may be older and slower to move, but when the time is right, we can still groove.

Between us, we have raised lots of children, even some grandchildren and possibly a sibling or two. We have held many types of jobs and had some wonderful careers. Now its our time to live the Golden Years, to travel and see the world. To volunteer and be helpers to all that we can, or be advisers, mentors, or just friends to as many people as we can. To be there for others in their time of need, to lend a helping hand or maybe just to hold their hand. To just sit and listen when someone needs to vent, or a shoulder to cry on when the world comes crashing in. We feel like we have gifts and talent and knowledge that we want to share.

Always consulting with the Lord to keep us on His path. We want to be there for anyone who needs us around. We want to be of service for all those who God wants to reach out to showing His love and compassion in our community. We want people to join us so we can make new friends or someone to have a cup of coffee with. Someone to sit with and study God's word, or maybe just to take you to a doctor's appointment or maybe a trip to the grocery store.

We want you to know there is always a smile at our front door for you. So lets meet and greet, eat and have fun, find places to go and events to attend. We don't want to be boxed up and put away because we are old. We have millions of things to impart and many things we can show to the young. So we kindly and lovingly invite you to come and get to know us. But membership is exclusively for 60-plus. Sincerely, The Green Door Team.

The Newlyweds

Joey and Alyssa—the wonders of a brand-new love. The first few months after you say I DO. You two have had the advantage of asking all of the questions that most newlyweds never do. Having a pandemic happening shortly after you were married added so much extra, uninterrupted time alone. No outside world putting pressure on you, no unwanted advice from outside forces. Just the two of you, all snug like a bug in a rug.

Getting to hear you both speak to the church was such a treat.

The love you both have for the Lord stands out like a huge searchlight in the sky. It is there for all to see and hear but more than that to enjoy. Alyssa, the many people I have heard over the years say I wasn't getting married and especially to him.

The Lord is up in heaven shaking His head saying, "But I picked you two for each other, so please get with my program."

Joey, your love of speaking and teaching others has been so evident since you were young. I'm also guessing from what I have heard you say, Alyssa, that the same holds true for you.

You both have had shining examples through out your whole lives of what God can and has done with your families. Sitting in church listening to you was so heartwarming and joy-filled. It was such a pleasure to hear your talk and get excited about the Lord. Watching your touching and smiling at each other as you talked showed the world the love the Lord has put inside of both of you for each other.

Joey, your calm demeanor as you talk about what you have done and what you want still to do makes up your calm and peace.

Alyssa, your joy and excitement that takes over when you start talking is wonderful to see and hear. Your little abbreviations when you talk adds that extra touch to your presentations, we can all relate to that.

This is just the start of a life that will have no bounds or borders, whatever the Lord leads you both to say or do will be done. You are such wonderful examples to young people of what the Lord can do for others if they will just follow Him. You two are such beacons in your walk with the Lord. I know that your future will just get bigger and bigger; it will even amaze you both what the Lord has in mind for the two of you.

You two will be a young up and coming power couple in the Christian ministry world. Soon millions of people will know who you are and what you stand for. The world is your oyster and it is just starting to open up. So hang on tight, because you have one fast-moving life ahead of you doing what the Lord leads you to do. May all of your wishes and heart-filled desires come your way as you walk your path with God.

I know that your parents are so proud of both of you. They can't keep the smiles off of their faces. May you always feel the Love of the Lord for you both and for those around you.

The Wonder of You

This is a song that Elvis Presley sang and I think that it has a
good message for us all.
When no one else can understand me
When everything I do is wrong
You give me love and consolation
You give me hope to carry on
And you're always there to lend a hand in everything I do
That's the wonder, the wonder of you
And when you smile the world is brighter
You touch my hand and I'm a king
Your love to me is worth a fortune
Your love for me is everything
I guess I'll never know the reason why you love me as you do
That's the wonder, the wonder of you
Like that song says, the Lord does understand us.
He's always there, holding our hands, even when we do wrong.
His love for us gives us the strength to carry on.
I know that I am in awe of the wonders of the Lord.
All the things He has done:
The sun, the moon, and all the stars.
All the land and mountains.
The animals, the food, the lakes and streams.
The planets, everything is because of Him.

Knowing that He did all of this,
but this is just a small portion of what He has done,
is continuing to do for us in the blink of an eye.
Knowing that we are His children
and how much He loves and cares for us.
That alone is worth a fortune.
It should bring peace and contentment to our lives.
We may never fully understand why He cares for us so much,
but knowing He does should bring the feeling
that we are always on His mind.
Just as He should always be on our minds.
Thanking Him daily for all the things He does for us
and all of the gifts and blessings He gives us daily.
For only by believing in Him
does our life make sense and have a purpose.

Those I Admire

Did you ever meet some people in your life who you admired?
Maybe it was the way they acted and treated people
Maybe it was the smile that you would always see
Maybe it was God's love you saw in them
My parents were loving and protective of us
My grandparents showed us unconditional love
All our aunts and uncles treated us as their own
My parents did struggle raising four kids four years apart
They taught us right from wrong
They taught us good from bad
The importance of family
They taught us to respect them and others
They taught us they were always there for us
I admired some of our neighbors who were kind to us
If we wanted some fruit from their trees, we just had to ask
They let us play games in their big yards
They treated us fairly as long as we did no wrong
They were thankful for the errands we ran for them
As I have grown up, I have met many people I admire
They are usually warm, compassionate people
They openly show people their caring about them
They are willing to give you advice if you ask
They treat you as they want to be treated
They build you up and encourage you to try new things
When you think about them it brings a smile to your face
They never judge you or put you down
They listen and love you just as you are
They know the good and bad and love you anyway

They are always just a phone call away
So when needed and you call they say hey
Such warm feelings you always get from them
These are the kinds of people that I admire
They all are warm people with really great hearts
So I'm wishing you lots of people for you to admire
Hopefully they will be religious people you will admire

Thoughts for 2018

Whether you are close or far away
The Lord is always with you. You simply have to pray
Just pick up His book and start reading away
When problems surround you,
raise up your hands to the man up above
Dear Lord, these problems I give you to take care of
Love Him and praise Him and honor Him each day
Thank Him for the blessings He gives us each day
Be thankful for all of the gifts that He has given us
Sit back and enjoy all the things that God has made
The moon and sky, water and land, birds and bees
Fish and game, flowers and grass everywhere
These are all things He made for us to share

Before you leave the house each day
here is a little prayer to say:

*Dear Lord, please watch over me and
everyone else on the road today,
and get us all to our destinations safely and accident-free.
I ask this in Your holy name, Amen.*

Treasure Jubilee

Your name is so unexpected but has come to stand for so much.

I don't think when your parents chose your name they ever thought that 2 1/2 months later it would mean something else.

For those of you who don't know Treasure, she was born much, much to early, so she is a preemie. She weighed in at a little over one pound and five ounces plus. She would fit in the palm of your hand. The medical and breathing problems that she has survived have been amazing. Her everyday existence has been and continues to be a Treasure.

Her life struggles from day to day have had her parents living on the brink. One day she is OK, the next day she is in crisis. Laughter and tears are what my parents' lives have been. Living in dread and hoping for miracles, which my heavenly Father has filled. The many, many people who constantly pray for her and her family.

Treasure might say: I am luckiest little girl, I have parents who love me to death and who I dearly love in return. I have wonderful siblings who come and visit me and pray for me all of the time. I have grandparents and lots of relatives and friends who love and pray for me.

I have inspired many people who read of all the struggles I have been through. My fighting spirit inspires them to fight harder for the things in their own lives. Just saying my name brings a smile to their faces. It has restored their faith and belief in the Lord. If not for all of His many miracles, I wouldn't be here.

The Lord has wonderful plans for Treasure and we are all waiting to see what they will be.

Treasure's doctors and nurses are finally talking about her going home. She and her family can't wait for that day to come. When she will be able to absorb all the love that will be surrounding her. The day she comes home will be a Jubilee (a special anniversary of an event) for all who love her and have prayed for her.

Treasure (a quantity of precious metals, gems or other valuable objects) that is what her name means.

Yes, she is one of the greatest treasures to her family and friends. I imagine that her future will continue to be a treasure. Her life will be an inspiration to people who are seeing a living Miracle. I feel that the Lord has special plans for her in her future life. Praying you will continue to grow in health and your faith will be your greatest treasure. May God bless you and love you every day of your life.

Thank you, Lord, for this beautiful Treasure.

Treasure's Journey

I came really early and my body was not matured. I weighed a little over a pound when I was born. So I live right now at the hospital in an isolette and I am on a ventilator to help me breathe. Each day a new obstacle comes up and needs to be overcome. Thanks to a wonderful God who loves me so dear. He takes away all of the obstacles that appear. He heals my body as each new problem appears. I have lots and lots of people praying for me every day. All of these people praying for me know my mom and dad and love us all dearly. I don't think when my parents named me Tresure, they realized that my daily struggles and improvements make me a treasure. My first three weeks make my life a treasure for sure.

Well, now I am one month old and I weigh two pounds, four ounces and I am 13.5 inches long. So hurrah for me! I'm growing for everyone to see.

Hooray! Now I'm 30 weeks old and weigh 39 ouces. I'm on my NIPPV now to help me breathe, my oxygen is coming down and I am growing in leaps and bounds. My mom finally got to hold me for the first time since I was born. She had to be at home healing from her surgery, so my dad took care of me. It was so warm and loving being back with Mommy where I belonged. Mommy loves me so much and I love her the same way. Mommy and Daddy trade off weeks with each other coming to be with me. So now Daddy is here and we love each other so much.

Daddy makes funny faces when they place me on his chest. I can't wait until I am full term and hopefully I will be big enough that I will get to go home with Mom and Dad and my siblings. My Heavenly Father is taking such good care of me until then.

Yeah! Great news. I weigh over 3 pounds now and get closer and closer to my gestation date. Mom and Dad can both be with me at the same time now. I am in heaven having them both here but I miss my one-on-one time with each of them. I took my ventilator out so they put me on a NIPPV to help me breathe. I am hoping that all goes well. Pray for me to do well on this.

Well, I weigh 4.5 pounds and I am 33 weeks old. I got off of the NIPPV and now I am on a bubble CPAP to help me breathe. The next step after this is pure oxygen just like you all breathe. My oxygen is way down just a little lower and I will be normal. My Father Above is taking miraculous care of me as He promised. Everybody has asked Him for this and He is delivering. Amen. Like the tortoise and the hare; slow and steady win the race.

Well, I am now 34 weeks and I weigh all of 5 pounds. I am just growing and growing. Heavenly Father, thank you for all the gifts You have given me. I am doing so well. I weigh five pounds, two oz and hopefully in two to three weeks I can go home. So this has been my journey so far. Mom will keep you updated in the future.

Thank you all for your prayers, but please keep praying for all of us after I get to go home. I'm sure they will be needed along with God's wondrous miracles to help me grow up to be a beautiful little girl. Three more weeks and I will be a full-term baby. Thank you, Lord.

When I get to go home I will miss the wonderful nurses who cared for me so dear and the good doctors who took such wonderful care of me. Thank you all so much.

We Never Walk Alone / Putting your Faith in God

In 1964, while crossing a street, I was struck by a car. I was tossed in the air and landed on the curb. I walked away with no broken bones or internal injuries. I know the Lord was with me, protecting me. Years later, I learned that I had a blood clot in that leg that calcified and turned into a piece of bone, which I had removed in 2012.

In 1994, I went to a neurosurgeon because I was having pain in my neck. He did an MRI and said that I had three disk problems and a bone spur that was pressing on my spinal column. He said that I needed to have surgery done, because if I ever was in a car accident, I could end up being a quadriplegic. At the time, I was not ready to undergo that type of surgery. I placed my life and my health in God's hands.

Ten years later, I started having tingling sensations going from my chest up into my neck area and face. I figured that this was a message from God that it was time to have my surgery done. I went back to my neurosurgeon and we settled on a date to do my surgery. My doctor is very conservative so he only repaired one disc with a plate and screws and removed the bone spur that was pressing on my spine. With God protecting me and guiding my doctor's hands, my surgery was completed with no complications and no side effects.

In 1999, when I had my yearly mammogram, it showed calcium deposits in my breast. My doctor went in and removed the calcium deposits. After this procedure, they did another mammo to make sure that they got it all. The mammo showed some of it was still there. The radiologist who read my mammo noticed a spot on my previous mammos that was getting smaller.

She asked the doctor to do a biopsy on that spot when he went back in to get the rest of the calcium out because she wanted to know why this spot was getting smaller, That biopsy came back as cancer. I went to the radiologist and thanked her for finding this spot.

God sent this special woman to intervene in my life and find this cancer so something could be done now. I had a mastectomy and all the surrounding tissue came back clear of cancer, so I did not have to have any chemotherapy or radiation treatments.

I thanked the Lord and told Him that my life was in His hands as to whether my cancer ever returned. If God had not intervened and put that doctor in my path, by the time someone else might have found this years later, it could have been stage four and I would not be here. That was 19 years ago and counting.

Putting your faith in God's hands can be the best thing you ever do. It can also be the scariest thing you ever do. But never fear—it is always the right thing to do. God loves us so much that trusting Him with our life is the greatest gift we can ever give Him. His face lights up every time we walk with Him. I am walking proof that walking in faith with God works.

What are You Grateful For?

I'm grateful for the air I breathe, a roof over my head,
and a bed to sleep on
I'm grateful for food on my plate and the clothes on my back
I'm glad that wringer washers and coal furnaces are long gone
I'm grateful that I live in a country where I can be free
I'm grateful for all the Lord has given us
I'm grateful that the Lord has been in my life
long before I realized it
I'm grateful His hands have been on me
guiding me since I was a child
I'm grateful I had a guardian angel always watching over me
That there was always someone there to hold me and love me
That God's love and protection is always with me
For His words that we can read and speak
I'm grateful that He is always ready to help me if I ask
I'm grateful that Jesus died for my sins and I am forgiven
I am grateful for all of my family and friends
I'm grateful for my church family and their friendship
But most of all I'm grateful to God
Grateful for Him always being in my life

What Do You Do After the Intimacy is Gone?

What do you do after it's all gone
You cry like you've never cried before
You rant and rave to no appeal
Thinking that this can't be real
No one to hold and cuddle with
Missing the time when you had it all
Wondering why it all went away
Never any answers no matter how hard you pray
Wondering how to fill your day
In hope that the pain will go away
The gaping hole inside your heart
How do you ever mend that part
The hardest part is they haven't gone away
So how do you deal with this every day
If you are not married it's an easy choice
But when you are married there isn't a choice
Hopefully you can find a way to carry on
Doing this will hopefully make you strong
Relying on the Lord to fill me up with all of His wonderful love

What God Wants from Us

God, if we have fear, come hold us near.
Fill us with Your calming grace.
Let us look upon Your smiling face.
Because our lives are going at such a crazy pace.
In this unbelievable time in the human race.
Let Your loving arms be our resting place.

Always remind us of Your faith in us. We are such gullible people easily swayed. Always forgetting whose life You gave that day. We need to stop each and every day to pray, asking You to guide our way. Keep us on your path and to never let us stray. Fill us with thoughts, messages and prayers to speak to others for them to relay on. Reading our Bible day after day, always believing and following in Your loving way.

Let us always remember that You come first in our life. Reading and believing in every verse. Hoping for the best and prepared for the worst. Some people feel like their lives have been cursed. But that all can change if you put God first.

Always take time to put the Lord in your life. That way, you will avoid all of the unnecessary strife. Trusting and believing in the Lord is such a delight. That way your walk in life will always be right.

Sit down and think what the Lord wants you to do. When you help others, you won't be blue. It will always fill up your soul so you feel new again. Try always to live your life by the Golden Rule. Trusting in God's word will keep us from being a fool.

Show God's love in everything you say and do. Always ask yourself what would the Lord want me to do. Showing kindness, compassion, and love should be your #1 rule. We are just a cog in

God's scheme for His world. We will never know what role we are to play in God's world. But if you are nudged to do something like write, sing, dance, or public speaking, just do it as it is probably the Lord knocking on your door. It may be just a little whisper or maybe a big roar so open the door. Step back and let the Lord come in. I can guarantee you that your life will feel His peace from within.

So always be helpful and kind. Love everybody all of the time. Think of others, not just yourself. Because you will never know if you just passed one of God's little test. Smile at everyone you see; the difference that will make you will never see. They will pass that smile along until no one feels alone. A simple deed will have repercussion beyond belief. Always think of the ruler of our life.

Where has the Time Gone?

It has been almost a year the tears have slowed
but not totally stopped.
Going through all of your stuff, sorting there was a lot,
it took a long time.
Finally starting to feel a little peace in my mind.
Starting to think what my future might be,
also wondering what everyone will think
Holding off making some decisions
because of what others might think.
Have to decide what I want to do with my life.
Enough time has gone by that I feel I can move on
But fear of people talking has me holding myself back
For now returning to our church you cannot do.
Right now still too many memories of Roger and you.
How you started this church and worked to make it grow.
All the joys and trials that you went through
starting up that church
So many memories to have to get through
When you are ready, you will come back
You have so many friends waiting for you here
and they all miss you so much
Roger, you are still so dearly missed

Will

A beautiful child of God. I never knew Will personally but met him today through his dad. I learned he was a loving child who radiated God's love. Will, you were one of two apples in your mother's and father's eyes. You were one of two reasons they got up every day. The pride they felt the day you were born was indescribable. Your grandparents beamed just as much as your Mom and Dad did when you were born. The way their eyes lit up when they held Jack and Will.

Such wonderful memories of the life that you had then. Holding him was like being touched by the Lord. He had the power to calm us when we held him, a gift our Heavenly Father gave to him. Even though he wasn't with us very long, he left us with a lifetime of memories to hold onto to. But suddenly something terrible happened and Will got diagnosed with severe medical problems. There were many struggles to endure, plus many good days and bad days too.

* * *

Then my Heavenly Father called me home to him. I was sad to go but I knew it was meant to be and I was going to be safe and loved by my Heavenly Father.

* * *

Thinking back on Will's time on earth is sad but it is also comforting, in its own way. Our hearts are broken leaving us so lost; our only comfort is the words and feelings our Father has bestowed on us.

* * *

My family has been so sad since I went to heaven. My Heavenly Father has been talking to my dad, trying to help him heal. He has also been there holding my mother when she cries.

* * *

You now have a better understanding of how our Heavenly Father felt when He sacrificed His son for our salvation. He is bestowing a father's love on you in the hope that it will bring peace to your life. He knows that Jack is still there for you two to lavish love on. Hoping that you being able to talk about me will bring you lasting peace in the future.

The Lord never gives us more than we can handle, but sometimes we wonder how we are going to handle what He has given us.

Worry and Fear

Isaiah 43:1 Don't fear for I have redeemed you. I have called you by name, you are mine. God commands us not to fear or worry.

Why then do we find it so hard to obey Him. We have read of all the things that Jesus did when He walked this earth. So why then do we still not believe in His word. We are such imperfect people trying to be better. But our imperfections keep leading us back to fear and worry.

I try to be analytical about things. Is my worrying going to change this problem. Most of the time the answer is NO, so logically we need to stop worrying. I try to just give it to the Lord to deal with.

I grew up with a mother who worried about everything, whether she could change things or not. So when I got older, I delayed telling her about an upcoming surgery because I knew that all she would do is worry until the surgery was done. So I would tell my older sister and when my surgery was done, she would tell my mother I had surgery and was well.

Since I was in Germany at the time, I knew that there would not be any phone calls fussing at me. I firmly believe that my mother's constant worrying caused her to develop cancer later on. My mother passed away before my 40th birthday from cancer.

I have refused to worry about things that I cannot change; that is the Lord's job. But we, as human beings, battle fear and worry all of the time. We go around thinking this is ours to fight alone and the Lord is sitting there, shaking His head, waiting for us to ask for His help.

We need to learn to give problems to the Lord and let Him handle those. He can make a difference while we never can. It doesn't mean that we are failures; it means that we truly believe in the Lord's word and that He will deal with things.

Like the song says, "Fear, he is a liar, because most of the time, that fear comes from the devil, who is constantly trying to break our faith and bring us back to him. His goal is to always make us doubt and fear; that way he is hoping to keep us from praying to the Lord for help.

Fear can be so paralyzing that it can cripple our lives. It causes us to mess up and lose our jobs, making us feel like failures. Sometime it leads us to drinking and drugs to try to mask this fear but that doesn't help. Or we withdraw into ourselves and shut out those we love. Sometimes that leads to the breakup of our marriage or relationship.

Some people get so down they take their own lives. When that happens, the devil is overjoyed because he has won. Don't do theses things.

Turn to the Lord, who is always there with open arms waiting for us and loving us. Let us rely upon His power and love to bring us through any situation. Like the saying goes: if He brings you to it, He will bring you through it.

Always praise and love the Lord, for He always loves us.

You Are My All

Heavenly Father, You are my everything. I know that I cannot do anything without You. You are all that I can be and all that I need in my life. Without You, Lord, I am nothing. You guide me every day in every way. You keep me from straying from Your path. You always show me the way to Your righteousness. You keep my heart focused on You, Your ways, and Your word that is written in the Bible.

You created this whole world in six days and on the seventh day, You rested. So I know how powerful You are, so there is nothing You cannot do. I know I need You in my life, but I don't know what things You want me to do. I witness people using my life experiences, hoping that someone can take away something from what I have said. I know that everything that I write is from You. I know that all of these words are Yours and I am just the servant to write them.

I know that my writing is a God-given gift from You. I wonder if this is my way of praising You. I know that some have the gift of speaking in tongues. I know that some other's gift is being able to hear You speak to them. I am profoundly desirous, of wanting to have these other gifts. Is it something that we have to earn or do we just need to ask the Lord to grant us these gifts. I sometimes feel lacking because I do not have these gifts. I pray that God will grant me more gifts. Until then I will work with all of the gifts I have. Thank you, Lord, for being my Savior.

I wish everyone could see how easy it is to have You in their lives. A simple, "Please, Lord, help me," is all it takes. He just wants us to ask for His help. So there are no more excuses. You just have to reach out to Him. Please don't delay. He is waiting for you and the end of time is getting shorter until He returns.

www.ingramcontent.com/pod-product-compliance
Lightning Source LLC
Chambersburg PA
CBHW072148270326
41931CB00010B/1928